Healthy Cooking

LOW CARB COOKBOOK

Healthy Cooking

LOW CARB COOKBOOK

Paul Morgan

AN OCEANA BOOK

This edition published by Silverdale Books,
an imprint of Bookmart Ltd., in 2006

Bookmart Ltd.
Blaby Road
Wigston
Leicester
LE18 4SE

This edition printed 2006

ISBN 1-84509-235-X

QUMHCLC

Manufactured in Singapore by
Pica Digital Pte. Ltd.
Printed in Singapore by
Star Standard Industries (Pte) Ltd

It is always sensible to consult your doctor before changing your diet regime, but it is essential to do so if you suffer from any medical condition or are taking medication of any kind. If you are concerned about any symptoms that develop after changing your diet, consult your doctor immediately. Information is given without any guarantees on the part of the author and publisher, and they cannot be held responsible for the contents of this book.

CONTENTS

INTRODUCTION

Low-carbohydrate diets have been very much in the news lately. There are a number of different versions, including the Atkins Diet and the South Beach Diet, and most of them demand that you should eat tiny amounts of carbohydrate for an 'induction period', introduce them at low levels after it, and obtain a large proportion of the calories that your body needs from protein and fat. There are two major drawbacks to such diets: first, they bring about significant weight loss in the short term, but seem to be ineffective over longer periods; second, there is no long-term research about their safety – and this is worrying when you consider that they go against everything that modern science knows about nutrition and its relationship to health. But this is a healthy eating cookbook, so in the pages that follow we are going to show you how to lose weight on diet that is never 'no carb', but is 'low-carb' – the carbohydrates that we advise you to limit in your diet are the unhealthy ones.

But what is a healthy diet? For 25 years or more, theories about what constitutes a healthy diet have chopped and changed. Take your heart and circulatory system, for example. First, all fat was considered to be bad for you – then it was found that some types of fat can protect your heart. Then butter was considered bad, while margarine was thought to be good for you – but after a while, scientists discovered that margarine contained substances called trans fatty acids, which are extremely bad for you. At the same time, all cholesterol was once considered dangerous, but now we know that one type of cholesterol is, in fact, very good for you.

Olive oil contains unsaturated fats, which increase the levels of beneficial HDL cholesterol while lowering the blood levels of harmful LDL cholesterol.

And for 17 of these 25 years, scientists tended to mock the insistent claims made by practitioners of fringe and alternative medicine to the effect that people could prevent cancer from developing if they ate the correct diet. But in 1997, the doubters were proved wrong, when the World Cancer Research Fund and the American Institute for Cancer Research (AIRC) published a joint study that was the culmination of 15 years of research. In it, they stated

> *'The panel found that . . . inappropriate diets cause around one-third of all cancer deaths . . . . [it] estimates that 30 to 40 per cent of cancer cases throughout the world are preventable by feasible dietary means'.*

Confused?

You could be forgiven if you are. But now, after years of research, scientists have a fairly clear picture of the relationship between nutrition and disease. The basic facts are now known: it is beyond question that by eating a healthy diet and avoiding some foods while emphasizing others you can not only lose weight but significantly reduce your chances of developing diseases of the heart and arteries and contracting many types of cancer. And a healthy diet emphasizes the importance of eating fewer unhealthy carbohydrates, choosing healthy carbohydrates, which help prevent disease, and reducing the amount of fat that you eat.

This book will show you how to eat healthily and lose weight. First we will look at what carbohydrates are and how they affect your body. Then we will show how the make-up of some foods can cause disease while the chemical basis of other foods can prevent it. Then you can choose from a range of mouth-watering, healthy recipes that utilise the appropriate carbohydrates. It may be a cliché, but like many clichés it is true: when it comes to your health, you really are what you eat!

TAKE MEDICAL ADVICE

Always consult your doctor before adopting a new diet regime. Many diets are unsuitable for people who suffer from certain conditions, or are taking medication. A low-carb, high-fat diet could, for example, be dangerous if you have a family predisposition to bowel cancer (because high fibre diets prevent against cancer, while red meat seems to promote it), or suffer from a kidney disorder (because your kidneys could be damaged by dealing with too many breakdown products of fat and protein).

WHAT ARE CARBOHYDRATES?

Carbohydrates are the body's primary source of fuel and are an essential part of a healthy diet. Without adequate supplies of them, the body has to look elsewhere for fuel, and using alternative resources – glycogen (stored sugar), fat and, ultimately, protein - can involve significant risks to health (see box, page 10). But that does not mean that all carbohydrates are either 'good' or 'bad'.

There are three types of carbohydrate: sugars, fibre, and starch, and all of them are built from molecules of sugar. They used to be described as 'complex' or 'simple' carbohydrates, depending on whether they were simple forms of sugar or consisted of linked (complex) forms of sugar, and it was believed that simple carbohydrates should be avoided and complex ones preferred.

Today this categorization is no longer used. Instead, nutritionists classify carbohydrates according to their glycaemic index, or 'GI' – as utilised in the GI diet. During the digestive process, carbohydrates are broken down into the simplest forms of sugar, and the glycaemic index measures how quickly this happens and so how fast levels of sugar in the blood rise – a high GI value means that the carbohydrate raises these levels very quickly.

The significance of this is that the pancreas starts to produce the hormone insulin in response to rising blood sugar levels, and this promotes the uptake of sugar by the body's cells and reduces sugar levels in the blood. If you continually eat foods with a high GI – and if you have a hereditary disposition to the problem or are overweight and inactive – the levels of both insulin and sugar in your blood remain high, and you develop what is known as insulin resistance (the body loses its sensitivity to insulin, so more and more is needed). This can not only lead to type 2 diabetes, but result in high blood pressure, low levels of 'good' cholesterol (see page 11) and an increased risk of heart disease. In short, low GI carbs are the best carbs, medium GI foods are reasonably good carbs – and high GI foods are bad carbs.

High or low?

In essence, whether a food has a high or low GI depends on how quickly its carbohydrates are converted to simple sugar during the digestive process. Foods that have not been processed – wholegrain foods – still contain their original fibre, which slows down the rate at which carbohydrates are converted to simple sugars and so also slows down the rate at which sugar enters the bloodstream; conversely, the carbohydrates in processed foods have already been partly broken down, meaning that their sugar enters the bloodstream relatively quickly.

However, the type of starch in the food is important, too: potatoes, for example, contain a starch that is broken down quickly during digestion. Other factors affecting the GI value are: ripeness – ripe fruit has a higher GI than unripe fruit; acidity – vinegar and lemon juice delay stomach emptying and so reduce the GI value; and the size of food particles – small particles are more easily absorbed by your body and increase the GI value.

High-fibre foods have a low GI value, but low GI foods also include foods such as soy and milk; medium ones include sugar, orange juice and oats; while high-GI foods include potatoes, rice, and wholemeal and white bread. It might seem a daunting prospect to exist solely on low-GI foods, but it is not necessary to do so. This is because eating low GI food reduces the GI value of high GI foods when they are eaten at the same time – if, for example, you eat cornflakes (high GI) with milk (low GI) your blood sugar levels will not go up as quickly – what is known as the overall 'glycaemic load' (GL) is reduced. In essence, the equation reads 'high GI + low GI = medium GI' – and low to medium GI is what you are aiming for on a low-carbohydrate, healthy eating diet.

PLUSES AND A MINUS OF EATING 'GOOD' CARBS

Maximizing the amount of low GI foods in your diet and minimizing the amount of high GI ones has numerous benefits:

- the slow breakdown of low GI foods during digestion and the gradual release of their sugars into your bloodstream means that you will not feel the 'sugar let-down' that comes when quick-release sugars are used up; in turn this means that you will not need to have another 'sugar hit' as quickly, so you will eat less – which means that you will lose weight (about 450 to 900 g a week)
- the slow release of sugars into your bloodstream increases your physical endurance
- low GI foods increase the body's sensitivity to insulin (see page 7), which reduces the risk of developing insulin resistance, and so diabetes and heart disease
- including a larger proportion of low GI foods means that you will reduce your intake of 'bad' saturated fats and trans fats (see page 11) and lessen the likelihood that you will develop heart disease
- there is some evidence that a low GI diet may help prevent some cancers
- so long as you choose low GI foods, you can snack between meals
- eating low GI foods leads to increased levels of the chemical serotonin in the brain – and serotonin makes you feel good
- low GI foods can form the basis of your diet for life, while the proscriptions of fad diets are much less easy to tolerate.

But, in case the benefits of eating a diet that emphasises low GI foods seems too good to be true, there is just one minus:

- healthy though they may be, even low-GI foods contain calories, so if you eat too many of them you will not lose weight: it is still necessary for you to control portion sizes.

CHECK THE LABEL

Food manufacturers are starting to note GI values on product labels, and the practice is likely to become more and more widespread. (In fact, the World Health Authority advises that GI values should be stated and that the values for 'complex carbohydrates' and sugars, which are used currently, are dropped.) But how do you interpret the figures?

The answer is that the maximum GI value, which is based on pure glucose, is 100, and that foods are said to have a low GI when the value is 55 or less; to be medium GI when the value is between 56 and 69; and high GI when the value is 70 or more. Remember that, ideally, you should stick to low GI foods; failing that, you should combine medium and low GI foods; and that if you ever eat high GI foods you should combine them with low GI ones.

A HEALTHY DIET

A diet low in 'bad' carbohydrates does have many health advantages, but cannot, on its own, be said to constitute a healthy diet. In the following pages, we are going to the link between nutrition and disease and show how you can improve your health by changing your diet. Essentially, it limits your intake of certain carbohydrates and fats, and maximizes your intake of life-preserving, 'good-carbohydrate' vegetables, fruits and grains.

Diet and blood pressure

Most people know that high blood pressure puts the whole circulatory system at risk, causing a build-up of fatty plaques in the arteries and leading to heart disease or a stroke. What is less well known is that it is also a risk factor for certain cancers – in particular, for kidney cancer. But what is high blood pressure, and what causes it?

Pressure points

The phrase 'high blood pressure' means that the force that blood exerts on the walls of arteries as it flows through them is higher than is normal. Blood pressure values are expressed as two figures, representing millimetres of mercury in an old-fashioned blood pressure measuring device (a sphygmomanometer): 120/80, for example, is considered normal. You are considered to have high blood pressure, and will be

FOODS TO CHOOSE

(Low glycaemic index carbohydrates)

Bran** and **porridge oats

Barley, buckwheat** and **bulgur wheat

Some fruits – apples, citrus, berries, peaches, pears, plums and rhubarb

Pasta

Some vegetables – avocados, aubergines, beans (runner and green), broccoli, cabbage, cauliflower, carrots, celery, courgettes, cucumber, leeks, onions, lettuce, mushrooms, olives, peas, peppers, spinach and tomatoes

FOODS TO USE SPARINGLY

(Medium glycaemic index carbohydrates)

Pure wheat cereals

Granary** and **whole-wheat bread

Basmati** or **long-grained rice, wild rice** and **couscous

Corn – cornmeal, corn oil and sweetcorn

Some fruits – apricots, bananas, melon, dried fruit, pineapples and mangos

Some vegetables – new potatoes, sweet potatoes, beetroot and artichokes

Honey

FOODS TO AVOID

(High glycaemic index carbohydrates

Breakfast cereals – cornflakes and sugar-coated cereals

White bread, cakes, biscuits, bagels, buns, muffins, pancakes** and **doughnuts

White** and **brown rice

Some fruits – dates, prunes and watermelon

Gnocchi

Some vegetables – broad beans, potatoes (when mashed, baked, fried or roasted), parsnips and swede

Sugar – table, glucose, treacle and molasses

Tomato ketchup

offered treatment for it, if your reading is 140/90 or higher. It is estimated that between 10 and 20 per cent of the population have high blood pressure, but many people do not know that they have it – there are often no symptoms, which is why it is sometimes known as "the silent killer."

White bread, cakes, puddings and biscuits should be avoided and replaced with fruit, yoghurts and low-fat desserts, as these contain more vitamins and minerals.

THE DANGERS OF BEING OVERWEIGHT

Being overweight brings with it the dangers of many health problems, including an increased risk of developing colonic and rectal cancer, but if you carry the extra pounds on your waist – in the classic 'beer belly' – you are far more at risk of heart disease or diabetes. In fact, men with waists of more than 101 cm (40 inches) and women with waists of more than 89 cm (35 inches) are at between double and quadruple the risk of developing them.

The reason is that fat that is stored around the stomach secretes hormones that play havoc with the production of insulin, the pancreatic hormone that controls blood sugar levels. As a result 'insulin resistance' develops, leading to diabetes, high blood pressure and high cholesterol levels. And a very successful – and healthy – way to lose weight is to adopt a diet low in high GI, 'bad' carbohydrates and high in low and medium ones.

WHY VERY-LOW-CARB DIETS CAN BE DANGEROUS

As we have said, carbohydrates are the body's principal source of energy. If you stop eating carbohydrates, or reduce your carb intake to a level that does not provide sufficient calories, your body will utilise its food stores. (Dietary fat provides more calories than carbohydrate, gram for gram, but it is difficult to eat sufficient of it to satisfy calorie requirements – and eating too much fat carries its own dangers [see page 11].)

In response, it will first break down glycogen (the form in which simple sugars are stored in the tissues). But there are limited stores of glycogen, so after a few days your body will move on to break down body fat and dietary protein and utilise it to provide energy – that is why people on the Atkins Diet, for example, often lose weight quickly (another reason is that the breakdown of glycogen releases a considerable amount of water from the tissues).

But while breaking down fat makes you look and feel better, doing so too quickly can have serious side-effects. The process involves the production of chemicals called ketones, and when there are too many ketones in the blood a potentially life-threatening condition called ketosis can develop. In extremes, this can cause coma and death; at medium levels, it can cause confusion and disorientation, and at lower levels, breath that smells of acetone, nausea and fatigue. (Dealing with excess ketones and the breakdown products of protein can also damage your kidneys.)

When the body has exhausted its fat stores, it starts to rely on dietary protein. Unfortunately, it is very hard to eat sufficient protein to satisfy the body's energy requirements, so the only remaining energy source is the protein that makes up its structures, such as the muscles.

Another problem for people on very-low-carb diets is that they are unlikely to absorb sufficient vitamins and minerals because they avoid the grains, fruit and vegetables that contain them – and vitamin supplements are not, scientists believe, as effective as natural vitamins derived from food (see page 15).

Atherosclerosis is the condition in which plaques (atheromata) form on the inner walls of arteries. The plaques consist of dead cells, fibrous tissue and calcium, among other things, but primarily contain cholesterol. They can cause the arteries to harden, narrow and become less flexible (arteriosclerosis), or block them. If atherosclerosis blocks the coronary arteries, which supply the heart with blood, the result will be a heart attack. Sometimes, too, pieces of plaque can break off (thrombi) and be carried around the circulatory system to block other, smaller blood vessels – if these supply blood to the brain, the result could be a stroke.

The nature of the link between atherosclerosis and high blood pressure is complex. Each condition can cause the other one, but generally both develop as a result of lifestyle factors and the natural processes of ageing (some people also have an inherited predisposition to them). Smoking, drinking excessive amounts of alcohol, obesity, high stress levels and the presence of other conditions, such as diabetes, play a major part in the development of both problems, but so, too, does your diet.

The culprits

The main dietary culprits when it comes to developing atherosclerosis and high blood pressure – and so some cancers – are saturated fats, trans fats, dietary cholesterol and salt. But some foods can actually prevent both problems. The trick is to know which foods to choose and which to avoid – and what follows will show you.

KEEP CHECKING

There are often no symptoms if you have high blood pressure – which is why it is known as the silent killer. But it is important that you know what your blood pressure is, so that you can take steps to reduce it if it is too high. In Britain, it is recommended that everybody asks their family doctor to check their blood pressure every five years, and more frequently with age; in the US, the recommendation is that blood pressure should be checked every two years over the age of 20.

FATS AND CHOLESTEROL

For many years, scientists believed that the cholesterol that you eat is the villain of the piece when it comes to heart disease. In fact, about 75 per cent of the cholesterol in your blood is manufactured by your liver, while only 25 per cent of it is in your diet. And the liver uses dietary fat to make cholesterol. When this was appreciated, the emphasis moved to eating a low-fat and low-cholesterol diet. But then it was discovered that it is not only the amount of fat in your diet that is important, but how much of which type of fat you eat – and there are three main types of fat: saturated fats, unsaturated fats and trans fats.

Saturated fats are found in meat, poultry, lard and whole-milk dairy products, such as cheese, milk, butter and cream, but high levels are also found in some vegetable oils, such as coconut and palm oil.

Unsaturated fats, which typically are liquid at room temperature, are found in plant and vegetable oils, such as olive, peanut, sesame, safflower, corn, sunflower, canola and soybean oil, and in avocados, oily fish (in the form or omega–3 fatty acid) and nuts and seeds.

Trans fats are man-made – a by-product of heating vegetable oils in the presence of hydrogen (which is why they are often referred to as 'hydrogenated vegetable oils' on product labels). They are found in commercial baked goods, such as biscuits, snack foods, processed foods and commercially prepared fried foods, such as crisps. Some margarines also contain high levels of trans fats, especially brands that are 'stick' margarines – spreadable ones have less high levels as they are less hydrogenated (hydrogenation makes the fat hard at room temperature).

Where cholesterol comes in

Your body needs cholesterol to function correctly – it is involved in the production of hormones, the body's chemical messengers, as well as bile and vitamin D, and is found in every part of the body. For this reason, it is manufactured in the liver – and the liver uses fats to make it. If you eat too much saturated fat, the liver produces too much cholesterol. And, unfortunately, cholesterol is a soft, waxy substance that can stick to the lining of blood vessels and obstruct them if there are high levels of it in the blood.

As we have seen, liver-produced cholesterol, and so the cholesterol that is ultimately the result of fat consumption, accounts for around 75 per cent of the cholesterol found in you blood. The remaining 25 per cent comes from the cholesterol you eat. Dietary cholesterol is found in eggs, dairy products, meat, poultry, fish and shellfish, but the highest levels are found in egg yolks, meats such as liver and kidneys and shellfish. Vegetables, fruits, nuts, grains and cereals contain no cholesterol.

Eggs can be cooked in many ways and are used in a lot of dishes. They contain essential proteins, but must be eaten in moderation as the yolks are paticularly high in cholesterol.

'Good' and 'bad' cholesterol

Cholesterol is carried around the body by chemicals called lipoproteins. There are two types: low-density lipoprotein (LDL) and high-density lipoprotein (HDL). If there is too much of the cholesterol carried by LDL, known as 'bad' cholesterol, plaque builds up on arterial walls. But HDL carries cholesterol away from the arteries to the liver, which breaks it down so that it can be excreted from the body; for this reason, HDL cholesterol is said to be 'good' cholesterol. It is now known that saturated fats, and, in particular, trans fats, increase the blood levels of harmful LDL cholesterol and lower levels of beneficial HDL cholesterol, while unsaturated fats have the opposite effect.

To sum up, then, a healthy diet, which helps prevent heart disease and some cancers, is one that has low levels of saturated and trans fats, and high levels of unsaturated fats.

FOODS TO CHOOSE

(Containing unsaturated fat)

Vegetable oils – pure olive, peanut, walnut, sesame, corn, soybean, sunflower and safflower oils

Avocados

Oily fish – salmon, mackerel, tuna, herrings and so on

Nuts and seeds

Spreadable, unsaturated margarine

FOODS TO USE SPARINGLY

(Containing saturated fat)

Whole-fat milk (skimmed milk is preferable)

Butter, cream, cheese, full-fat yoghurt (low-fat is preferable), ice cream

Meat – beef, lamb and pork

Poultry – battery-farmed chicken (free-range is preferable), goose, duck and turkey (wild game, such as rabbit, wild duck and venison, is better)

Lard

Eggs (especially ones from battery-farmed chickens)

Coconut oil and palm oil

FOODS TO AVOID

(Containing trans fats)

Ready-made commercial foods – cakes, biscuits and snack foods

Processed foods – sausages, pâté, scotch eggs, pies and so on

Commercially prepared fried foods – crisps, battered fish and chips

Hard margarine

FOODS TO USE SPARINGLY

(Rich in dietary cholesterol)

Organ meats – liver and kidneys

Eggs (especially ones from battery-farmed chickens)

Shellfish

Red meat

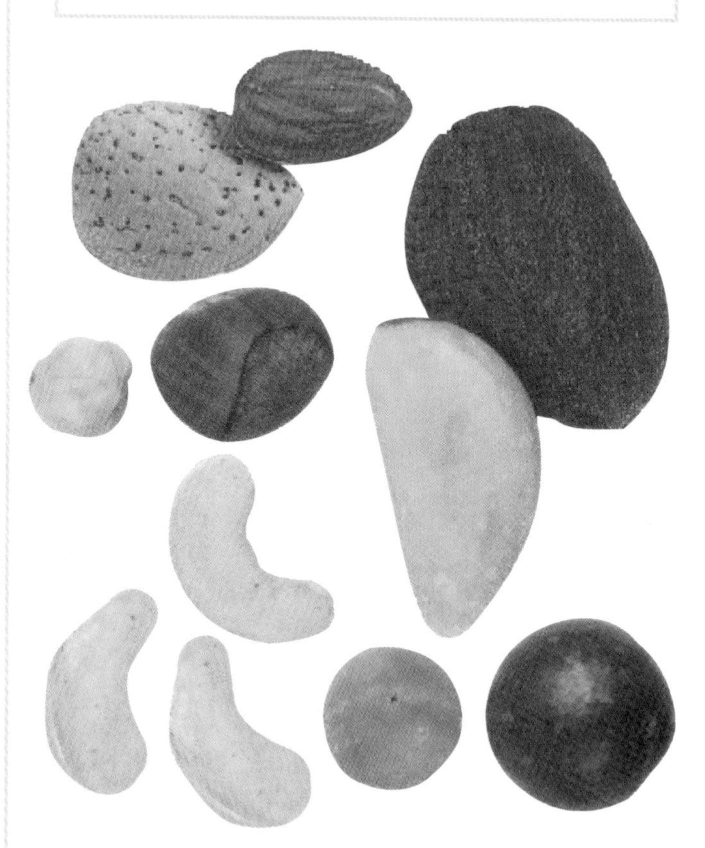

Nuts contain unsaturated fats and provide a variety of vitamins and minerals including vitamin B2, selenium, magnesium and vitamin E.

PROTEIN

Protein, made up from chemicals called amino acids, makes up the building blocks of all our body's tissues except stored fat. You need to eat a certain amount of protein every day – a minimum of one gram for every kilogram of body weight – to prevent the body from starting to break down tissue. And you need more than that if you want to build up healthy muscles and bones. The trouble is that if you eat large amounts of foods that are high in protein, as you are urged to do when on some of the high-profile low-carb diets, you are likely to put your cardiovascular system at risk – unless you choose protein sources that are low in saturated fat.

It is easy to get enough protein in your diet in Western industrialized societies, though hard to do so in developing countries. But the quantity of protein you eat is not the whole story. What is important is that you eat a variety of amino acids, which means protein from a variety of sources. This does not mean that it is essential to eat steaks, for example, because you can obtain a full range of proteins from vegetable and fruit sources, if you are a vegetarian. Variety is the watchword.

Chicken, preferably free range, is high in proteins but remember to remove the skin as this is just fat.

FOODS TO CHOOSE

('Good' protein – lower in saturated fats)

Vegetables – beans, brown rice, lentils, millet and pulses

Soybeans

Nuts – brazil, peanuts and pine nuts

Seeds – sesame

Free-range chicken *and* ***turkey*** *(but remove the skin)*

Locally sourced lean cuts of non-intensively reared meats – beef, lamb, pork and veal

Free-range chicken eggs *(but not duck or goose eggs)*

SALT

The more salt you eat, the more your body retains fluid, and the more fluid there is, the harder your heart has to work to pump blood around your body. And the result of this increase in the heart's work rate is high blood pressure and the risk, over time, of developing heart failure. High levels of salt in your diet are also linked to the incidence of certain cancers – in particular to stomach cancer.

Doctors recommend that our daily intake of salt should be less than 6 grams – about a teaspoonful. Even less salt than this is recommended for those who already have heart problems. The level is lower for children, too: up to 6 months old, it is less than 1 gram; between 7 and 12 months it is 1 gram; between 1 and 3 years it is 2 grams; between 4 and 6 it is 3 grams; and between 7 and 10 years it is 5 grams.

Hidden salt

The 6 gram target sounds an easy enough one to achieve, but in fact it is very tall order. The reason is that this target refers to our total salt intake, not just to the salt that we add to our food, and there is a considerable amount of salt hidden in the foods many of us eat. Processed foods are mainly to blame – in fact, researchers estimate that around 75 per cent of our salt intake comes from them.

The only way to check which processed foods are high in salt is to read product labels carefully. It is easy to come unstuck when you do this, however, because some labels do not refer to the product's salt content but to its sodium content (salt is made up of sodium and chloride). The two values are not the same – in fact, you have to multiply the sodium value by 2.5 to obtain the real salt content.

Reducing your salt intake

If you cut down on salt, your blood pressure will fall within weeks, even if it was not too high in the first place. And that means that your risk of developing heart disease, having a stroke or developing certain cancers will also fall.

Many people think that their food will lack taste if they cut down on salt, but this is a myth. You may find that your diet is a little bland for the first week or so, but your taste buds soon adapt. Adopt these salt reduction strategies and you will find the process much easier.

CALCULATE YOUR SALT INTAKE

If you must eat processed foods – and it can be hard not to – try to make sure that you stay within the recommended daily intake of 6 grams of salt. Read a product's label to find the number of grams of salt in 100 grams of the contents. If the quantity of sodium is given, multiply by 2.5 to calculate the actual salt content. (If the value is given in milligrams, or 'mg' divide by 1,000 to convert it to grams.)

Then look for the total weight of the contents, or estimate the proportion of them that you intend to use. Divide the weight that you will use by 100, then multiply by the number of grams of salt in each 100 grams and you will discover how much salt you will eat. The results can be surprising: one small (200g) tin of baked beans can contain as much as 1.7 grams of salt – just under a third of your total recommended intake; one slice of white, refined bread contains 0.61 grams of salt – so just the bread making up a lunchtime sandwich could well account for just under a fifth of your total recommended daily salt intake.

FOODS TO AVOID

All types of salt – table, rock, sea and garlic
Obviously salty foods – anchovies, salted nuts and ready-salted crisps

FOODS TO USE SPARINGLY

(High in salt)
Commercially made foods – biscuits, supermarket bread, cheese biscuits and crisps
Ready-made meals – including pasta, pizzas, curries and Asian cuisine
Tinned foods – baked beans, spaghetti, meats and vegetables
Preserved and smoked foods – bacon, ham, pickles, spiced sausage, stock cubes and sauces

SALT SUBSTITUTES

Some people find that their food tastes a little bland when they switch to a low-salt diet, and even though their taste buds will adapt within a few weeks some people find that they need a little help to make the change. A number of salt substitutes are on the market, but these contain part sodium and part potassium and in certain circumstances it is possible to overload your body with potassium – consult your doctor before using a commercial salt substitute.

Make your own

This recipe for a salt substitute relies on the principle that a sour flavour is a good substitute for a salty one. It uses the grapefruit peel (or lemon or orange peel, for a weaker taste) and citric acid crystal. Also known as 'sour salt' and 'lemon salt', these can be found in the baking section of supermarkets or in delicatessens.

Ingredients

- the peel of 1 grapefruit
- 1 tbsp ground allspice
- 1/2 tbsp citric acid crystals

Makes 3 tablespoons

Method

1 Peel the grapefruit as thinly as possible, then scrape away all the white parts. Dry the peel overnight near a source of heat.

2 Grind the dried peel in a coffee grinder or spice grinder, then combine it with the other ingredients. Put the mixture into a well-sealed bottle and shake well to mix. Store in a dry place.

Variations

Add a tablespoon of freshly ground black pepper to the mixture to make it into citrus pepper, an ideal seasoning for meat.

- **Avoid** processed foods
- **Check** the salt levels of all commercially prepared foods, including everyday products such as bread
- **Throw** away your salt shaker
- **Make** your own salt-free stocks and sauces
- **Use** alternative seasonings, such as lemon juice, herbs and vinegar
- **Eat** fresh fruit (bananas and avocados in particular) and vegetables: the potassium they contain helps counter the effect of dietary salt
- **Do** not switch to sea salt, rock salt or garlic salt – they are not different to normal salt
- **Ask** your doctor whether salt substitutes are suitable for you.

DIET AND CANCER

Contrary to popular belief, carcinogens (cancer-causing chemicals) in the diet are only very rarely a cause of cancer. The 15-year analysis of statistics relating to food intake and diet undertaken by the AICR has demonstrated that in a hugely significant proportion of cancer cases, the changes are the result of eating an unhealthy diet. Unfortunately, nobody knows for certain why this should be – perhaps ongoing research will provide the answer.

Here is a summary of the main findings of the AICR's study linking a reduction in the risks of specific cancers to dietary measures – as you will see, high-fibre vegetables and fruit are preventive against a number of types of cancer:

- **Lung cancer**: the most common cause of lung cancer is tobacco smoking, but a diet rich in vegetables and fruits may prevent between 20 and 33 per cent of cases in both smokers and non-smokers
- **Stomach cancer**: diets high in vegetables and fruits, and low in salt, together with the routine use of freezing and refrigeration of perishable foods may prevent between 66 and 75 per cent of cases
- **Breast cancer**: a diet rich in vegetables and fruit, an appropriate body weight and an avoidance of alcohol may prevent between 10 and 20 per cent of cases (more if this diet is adopted early in life)
- **Bowel cancer**: a diet high in fibre and vegetables and low in meat and alcohol may, together with regular exercise, prevent between 66 and 75 per cent of cases
- **Mouth and throat cancer**: a diet high in vegetables and fruit, and low in alcohol consumption may – in the absence of tobacco smoking – prevent between 30 and 50 per cent of cases
- **Liver cancer**: avoidance of alcohol (and of aflatoxins, found in a mould that grows on some nuts) may prevent between 33 and 66 per cent of cases.

The message seems fairly clear: if you smoke, stop now; moderate your alcohol intake; cut down on the amount of meat you eat; and emphasize 'good-carbohydrate' vegetables and fruit in your diet. And it is particularly important that you take these steps if you have a family history of cancer, because genetic predisposition is a major risk factor for developing cancer.

Luckily, an anti-cancer diet is the same as the diet that doctors and nutritionists recommend for healthy living, and it is this same diet that can prevent numerous other conditions, such as high blood pressure, heart disease and diabetes. It relies on limiting your intake of 'bad' carbohydrates and fats, and maximizing your intake of life-preserving vegetables, fruits and grains. In the following pages we will show you how to do just that – starting with a look at the chemicals, obtainable in a healthy diet, that actually prevent cancer from developing.

ANTIOXIDANTS, VITAMINS AND MINERALS

Many of our bodily structures can be damaged by the presence of what are known as 'free radicals' – technically speaking, these are atoms that have unpaired electrons. The most common free radical is radical oxygen, which can damage cells, causing them to develop cancerous changes, and increase the likelihood that cholesterol forms fatty plaques in arteries, leading to heat disease.

When this was realized, in the 1990s, nutritionists started to look at the antioxidants, which combat radical oxygen and so help prevent cancer and heart disease. These are known as 'phytochemicals', which literally means 'plant chemicals', and the most important antioxidants amongst them are vitamins C and E, beta-carotene (a precursor to vitamin A) and lycopene. Soon antioxidant supplements became increasingly popular, and today some 30 per cent of Americans take them. Unfortunately, they do not reduce the risks of cancer, heart disease or stroke, as a series of studies, and meta-studies (that is, studies of studies) have shown.

Nevertheless, it has been shown that a diet that is high in antioxidants is protective against cancer and heart disease. The answer to this conundrum is thought to be that in practice the effect of dietary antioxidants relies on the interaction between the antioxidants and other dietary ingredients: minerals, perhaps, or fibre. So it is important to eat a diet rich in antioxidants – that means richly coloured fruit and vegetables that contain chemicals called flavonoids, such as apricots, blueberries, bilberries, broccoli, carrots, mangos, peppers and spinach, and, in particular, tomatoes (though these should be cooked to release maximum quantities of flavonoids). And, just to show that a healthy diet need not be without its luxuries, there are high levels of flavonoids in both dark chocolate and red wine – though both should be enjoyed in moderation.

Vitamins and minerals

Every one of our body's systems need vitamins and minerals to function. Vitamins act as catalysts, initiating and controlling chemical reactions in the body, while minerals also play a vital part in body chemistry. Only small amounts of them are needed – they are known as micronutrients – and they must be obtained from our diet, because the body cannot manufacture them. If you follow the rules for healthy eating given in this book, and take a multivitamin supplement every day, as a precaution, you should absorb all the vitamins and minerals that your body requires. (Doing so is particularly important on a low-carb diet, because you may not be absorbing sufficient micronutrients in the food you eat.) But sometimes the way that we treat and cook food reduces its content of micronutrients. Follow these rules to make sure that you can meet your body's requirements.

- **Avoid** processed foods, and canned foods in particular, because these can be low in vitamin content.
- **Always** use fresh or frozen fruit and vegetables, because vitamin levels decrease as these foods age. It is not generally realized that freezing preserves vitamin content, but chilling fruit and vegetables in a refrigerator before heating them can reduce levels of vitamins such as vitamin C and folic acid by up to 30 per cent. Remember that frozen vegetables – peas, especially – are often more vitamin-rich than fresh ones, because they are frozen immediately after being picked.
- **Keep** all foods away from heat, light and air, all of which reduce levels of vitamin C and the B vitamins. Store vegetables in airtight bags.
- **Use** the skin of fruits and vegetables wherever possible and avoid trimming them too much. Instead of peeling, wash or scrub them – most of the nutritional value of fruits and vegetables is contained in the skin or the area underneath it.
- **Keep** the water you have used to cook vegetables and use it as a base for stocks or sauces – otherwise you will lose the valuable vitamins and minerals that have leached into the water.
- **Take** a daily multivitamin supplement – it can be hard to obtain sufficient quantities of some vitamins, such as B12 and folic acid from your diet; and fibre-rich foods contain chemicals called phytates, which can bind with some minerals and interfere with their absorption. But think of it as a nutritional safety net, rather than as a substitute for healthy eating.

These brightly coloured peppers contain antioxidants that help protect against cancer.

VITAMIN- AND MINERAL-RICH FOODS

(NB Pre-menopausal women and women taking HRT should eat more of foods containing vitamins that are depleted by the female hormone oestrogen.)

Vitamin A (antioxidant)
Retinol: butter, cod liver oil and cheese
Beta-carotene: apricots, cantaloupe, carrots, kale, peach, peas, spinach and sweet potatoes

Vitamin B1
Beans, brown rice, milk, oatmeal, vegetables, whole grains and yeast (depleted by alcohol, caffeine, exposure to air and water, food additives and oestrogen)

Vitamin B2
Eggs, fish, meat, milk, vegetables and whole grains (depleted by alcohol, caffeine, oestrogen and zinc)

Vitamin B3
Avocado, eggs, fish, meat, peanuts, prunes, seeds and whole grains (destroyed by canning and some sleeping pills; depleted by alcohol and oestrogen)

Vitamin B5
Bran, eggs, green vegetables, meat, whole grains and yeast (destroyed by canning)

Vitamin B6
Avocado, bananas, cabbage, cantaloupe, fish, milk, eggs, seeds, and wheat bran (destroyed by alcohol, heat, oestrogen and processing techniques during production of commercial food)

Vitamin B folic acid
Apricots, avocados, beans, carrots, green vegetables, melons, oranges and wholewheat (destroyed by commercial food processing techniques, cooking and exposure to water and air; depleted by alcohol)

Vitamin B12
Dairy products, fish and meat (depleted by alcohol, exposure to sunlight and water, oestrogen and sleeping tablets)

Vitamin C (antioxidant)
Broccoli, cabbage, cauliflower, citrus fruits, green peppers, spinach, tomatoes and potatoes (destroyed by boiling, exposure to air, and carbon dioxide and long storage; depleted by alcohol, aspirin, oestrogen, stress and tobacco)

Vitamin D
Cod liver oil, dairy products and oily fish (depleted by lack of sunlight)

Vitamin E (antioxidant)
Almonds, broccoli, eggs, kale, oats, olive oil, peanuts, soybeans, seeds, spinach, and wheat germ (destroyed by commercial food processing techniques, freezing, heat, oxygen and chlorine; depleted by smoking and use of contraceptive pills)

Vitamin K
Broccoli, cod liver oil, eggs, green vegetables, live yoghurt, tomatoes and whole grains

Magnesium
Bitter chocolate, brown rice, nuts, soybeans and wholewheat (depleted by caffeine and stress)

Zinc (antioxidant)
Eggs, meat, mushrooms, yeast and whole grains (inhibited by caffeine and smoking)

Potassium
Avocados, bananas, dried fruit, green vegetables, nuts and potatoes (lost in diarrhoea and sweat)

Selenium (antioxidant)
Broccoli, onions, tomatoes, tuna and wheat germ

TOO MUCH CAN BE DANGEROUS

Many people take high doses of vitamin supplements, without having taken medical advice. But doing so can be dangerous, because in many cases the effects of high doses are not known, and in some cases the effects have been confirmed to be dangerous. For example, it was once thought that vitamin E in very high doses might help prevent heart disease, but several studies have failed to show this and a recent study suggests that they may make heart failure more likely. And the list goes on: too much calcium can lead to lethargy, confusion and coma; excess vitamin B6 can cause a nerve disorder that leads to loss of feeling in the arms and legs; too much beta-carotene can increase the risk of contracting lung cancer in smokers; high doses of vitamin A can increase the risk of cardiovascular disease and can damage your liver; excessive doses of vitamin C can cause abdominal pain, nausea and diarrhoea; and so on.

The message is clear: do not take high-dose vitamin supplements unless they have been prescribed by your doctor – you can obtain all the antioxidants, vitamins and minerals you need by eating a healthy diet and taking a daily multivitamin and mineral supplement.

THE VALUE OF FIBRE

Our bodies cannot digest some of the food that we eat, and it is this indigestible material that is known as dietary fibre – it comprises the walls of plant cells. But even though fibre cannot be considered a nutrient, it has a considerable impact on your health. For example, it has now been shown (after some previous inconclusive studies) that increasing your fibre intake to the recommended level of between 20 and 35 grams a day (most people eat considerably less than this), as part of an overall healthy diet, can significantly reduce the risk of developing cancer of the bowel (see page 15).

That is not all. Importantly, it also significantly reduces the risk of developing heart disease and diabetes and suffering a stroke. This happens because one type of fibre can also lower the levels of cholesterol in your blood – which will lower your blood pressure (see page 8) and reduce your risk of developing other cancers, too.

There are two types of fibre: insoluble and soluble (the latter is so-called because it forms a gel when mixed with liquid). Insoluble fibre plays the main part in promoting bowel function and protecting against bowel cancer, and high levels of it are found in foods such as whole-wheat bread, wheat cereals, rice, barley, grains, cabbage, carrots and so on. But it is soluble fibre that reduces blood cholesterol – though it is not clear how it does this. It is found in oats, oat bran, oatmeal, peas, beans, barley and fruits – and, conveniently, foods containing soluble fibre contain 'good' carbs.

Foods containing soluble fibre include beans and chickpeas. These provide dietry fibre, as well as reducing blood cholesterol.

Five a day

So it makes sense to increase your intake of foods rich in fibre, and especially of those rich in soluble fibre – generally, it is recommended that you should eat five portions of fibre-rich fruit and vegetables a day. Make sure that you read labels carefully, though, because some commercial products that claim to be rich in fibre in fact contain very little of it.

FOODS TO CHOOSE

(High in soluble fibre)

Oatmeal and oat bran

Lentils, beans and peas

Apples, bananas, blueberries, oranges, pears and strawberries

Sweetcorn, spinach, spring greens and broccoli

Nuts – almonds, brazil, cashews, hazel, peanuts, pecan, pistachio and walnuts

Seeds – sesame, sunflower and pumpkin

FOODS TO USE

(High in insoluble fibre)

Whole grains – bran, wheat, couscous, brown rice, bulgur and barley

Whole-wheat and granary bread

Whole-wheat pasta

Whole-wheat flour

Wholegrain breakfast cereals

Fruit – both fresh and dried

All vegetables – but especially Brussels sprouts, carrots, cabbage, okra, parsnips, sweetcorn, courgettes, cucumber, celery, tomatoes and unpeeled potatoes

Vegetables are a good source of vitamins and minerals, and fibre. and you need to eat plenty to sustain a healthy and beneficial diet.

Seeds, including sesame, sunflower and pumpkin, are an excellent source of fibre. They can be used as an ingredient in meals, or can be eaten by themselves as a healthy snack.

STRIKING A BALANCE

It is easy to decide which foods you should eat, but more difficult to decide how often to eat them. It is also hard to strike a nutritional balance between foods so that you obtain all the nutrients that your body demands in the correct quantities, yet protect your heart and arteries at the same time. And you will have noticed already from the tables in this book that certain foods are 'good' in the sense that they contain substantial quantities of a desirable ingredient, but 'not so good' in that they contain less desirable ingredients. So how do you do it?

The healthy eating pyramid shown on the opposite page indicates how often you should eat the different food groups. For instance, while certain foods are important as part of a balanced diet, they need to be eaten in moderation because of the health dangers associated with overindulgence.

Eating a balanced, nutritious diet that is low in unhealthy carbohydrates is a challenging task, but the recipes in this book show that it is achievable. And once you have tried these delicious recipes, and have felt the health benefits that they bring, you are sure to become a true convert to healthy cooking.

EXPLAINING THE SYMBOLS

SOLUBLE FIBRE

HIGH

MEDIUM

LOW

UNSATURATED FAT

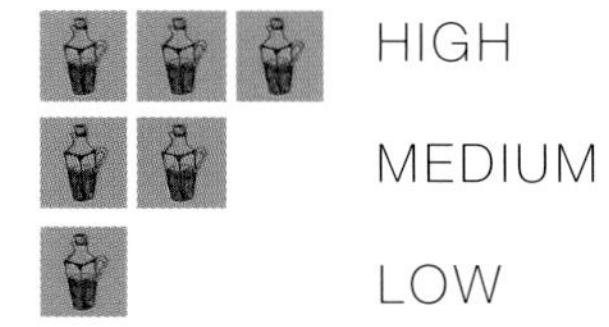

HIGH

MEDIUM

LOW

PROTEIN

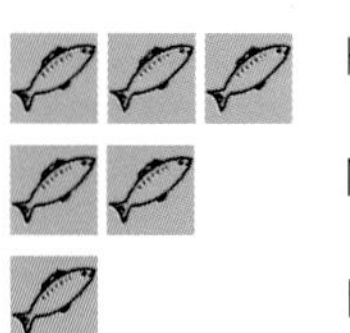

HIGH

MEDIUM

LOW

CHOLESTEROL

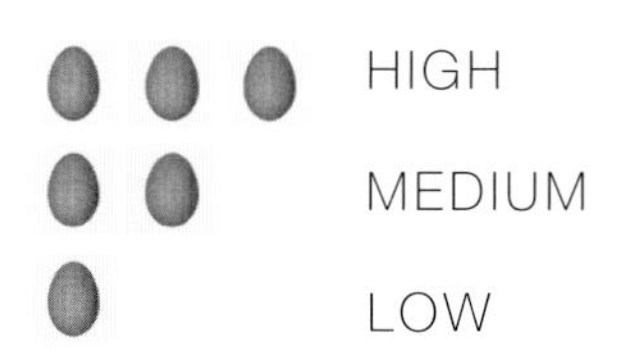

HIGH

MEDIUM

LOW

ANTIOXIDANT

HIGH

MEDIUM

LOW

CARBOHYDRATE

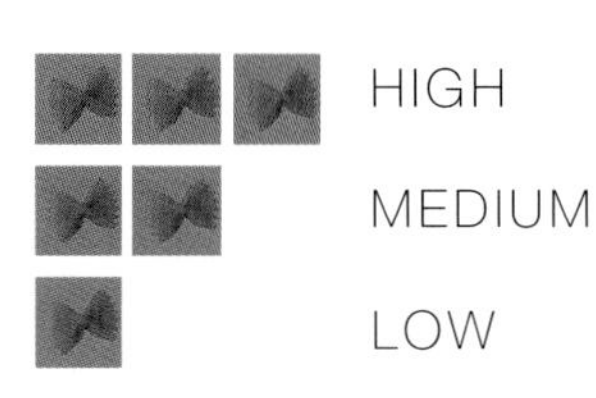

HIGH

MEDIUM

LOW

SATURATED FAT

HIGH

MEDIUM

LOW

INSOLUBLE FIBRE

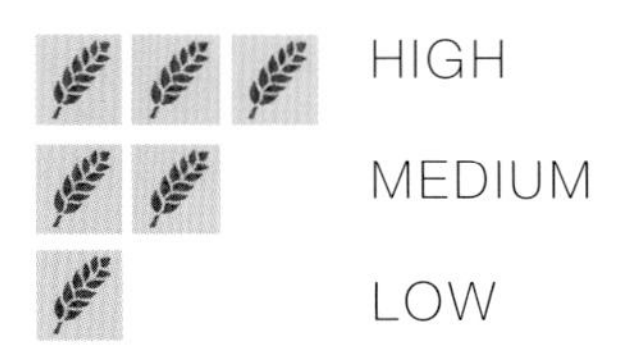

HIGH

MEDIUM

LOW

HEALTHY EATING PYRAMID

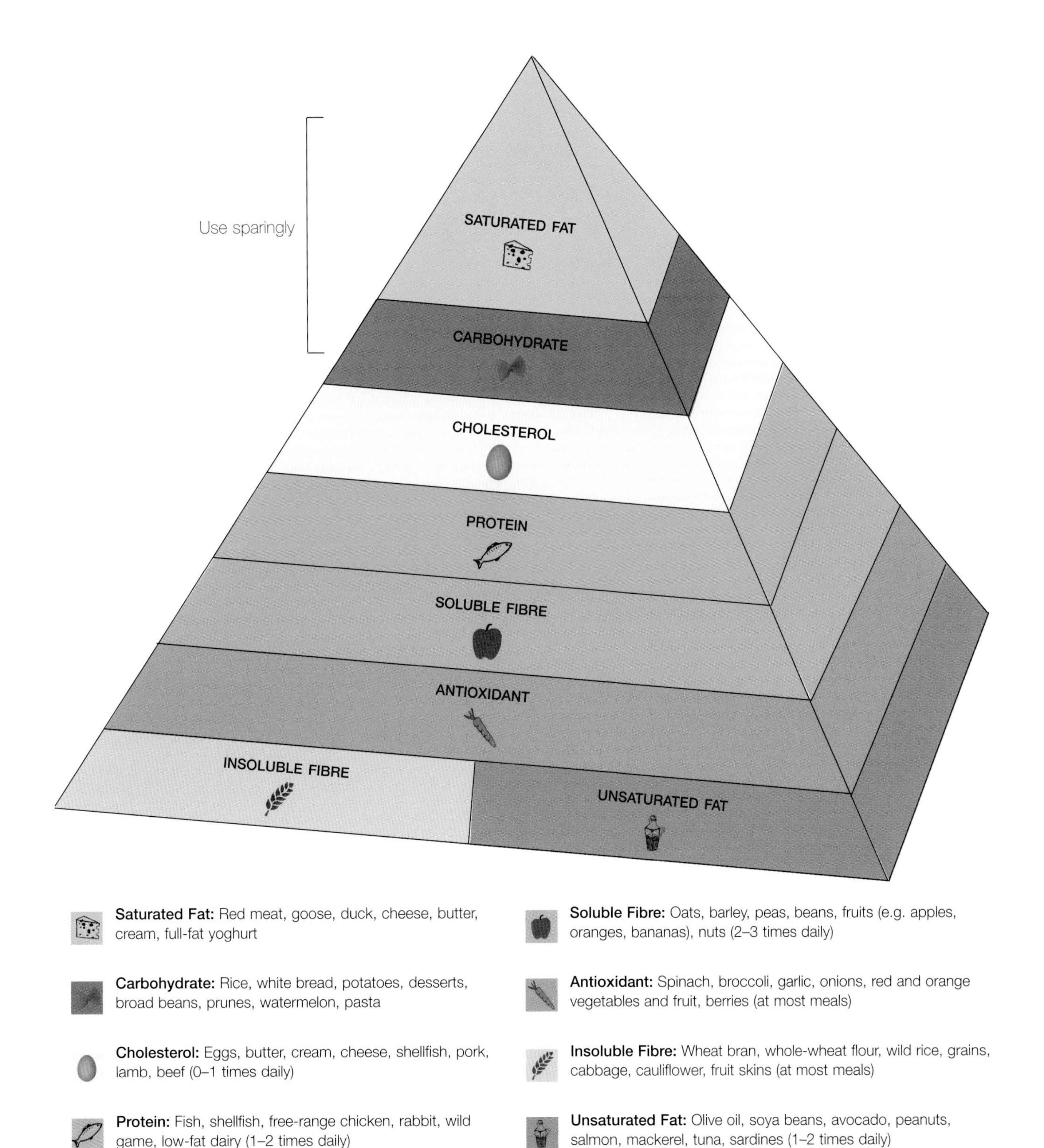

Saturated Fat: Red meat, goose, duck, cheese, butter, cream, full-fat yoghurt

Carbohydrate: Rice, white bread, potatoes, desserts, broad beans, prunes, watermelon, pasta

Cholesterol: Eggs, butter, cream, cheese, shellfish, pork, lamb, beef (0–1 times daily)

Protein: Fish, shellfish, free-range chicken, rabbit, wild game, low-fat dairy (1–2 times daily)

Soluble Fibre: Oats, barley, peas, beans, fruits (e.g. apples, oranges, bananas), nuts (2–3 times daily)

Antioxidant: Spinach, broccoli, garlic, onions, red and orange vegetables and fruit, berries (at most meals)

Insoluble Fibre: Wheat bran, whole-wheat flour, wild rice, grains, cabbage, cauliflower, fruit skins (at most meals)

Unsaturated Fat: Olive oil, soya beans, avocado, peanuts, salmon, mackerel, tuna, sardines (1–2 times daily)

HOW TO COOK HEALTHILY

There is little point in choosing healthy ingredients and recipes if you cook them in a way that is in itself unhealthy. It is important to choose cooking methods that not only help reduce cholesterol and saturated fats and keep the calorie count low, but maximize the nutritional value of each dish. These techniques are effective, but may require a little practise:

- **Baking** – good for vegetables, fruit, poultry and lean meat, as well as for puddings; you may need a little extra liquid
- **Braising or stewing** – brown first, on top of the stove, then cook in a small quantity of liquid; if you leave the dish in a refrigerator you can remove the chilled fat and then reheat it
- **Grilling** – on a rack, so that fat can drain away, and not in a direct flame
- **Microwaving** – place the food between two paper towels to drain fat away while it cooks
- **Poaching** – in a covered pan of the correct size, so that you use the minimum liquid
- **Roasting** – on a rack so that the food does not sit in fat; baste with fat-free liquids, such as wine or lemon juice
- **Sautéing** – use a high heat and a small amount of non-stick cooking spray, or just cook without spray if you have a good-quality non-stick pan
- **Steaming** – in a perforated basket over simmering water; add seasoning to the water for extra flavour
- **Stir-frying** – in a wok, using a small amount of non-stick cooking spray or a tiny amount of olive oil.

You can also increase flavour, reduce fat and salt content and make the most of your ingredients' nutritional value if you

Remember to:

- **Avoid** cooking methods that char food, such as barbecuing or grilling over a direct flame – charring produces carcinogens
- **Check** labels for common ingredients, such as soy sauce, baking soda and monosodium glutamate – these all contain high levels of sodium and should be used very sparingly, if at all
- **Make** your own stock rather than using pre-prepared cubes, which can be high in salt and may contain gluten
- **Steam** vegetables, for preference, in order to maximize both their flavour and nutritional value
- **Cook** lightly to preserve vitamin content (but cook meats and other foods that may harbour disease-producing organisms thoroughly)
- **Choose** extra virgin olive oil and vinegar rather than salted, pre-prepared salad dressings
- **Wash** canned vegetables before use – by doing so you can substantially reduce their salt content
- **Use** only one egg yolk when making scrambled eggs or omelettes, but mix in two or three extra egg whites
- **Trim** as much fat as you can from meat before you cook it and remove the skin from poultry
- **Choose** lean, low-fat meats, such as game (but, again, remember to remove the skin) and venison
- **Drain** oil from canned fish and rinse the fish in water before you use it
- **Use** herbs, wine and freshly ground pepper to enhance flavours; remember that a dash of vinegar or lemon juice will not only enhance flavour but reduce the GI rating of other ingredients.

Many different herbs and spices can be used to flavour your cooking instead of using salt, so be adventurous.

Soups can be made from nearly anything, and if made from scratch using fresh meat and/or vegetables, are full of wholesome nutrition.

MAKE YOUR OWN STOCK

Many stock cubes contain high levels of salt and low levels of nutrients. But nothing could be more simple than making your own stock, and if you make it in large batches you can freeze it for later use. You can use your stock as the basis for a delicious soup – serve it with a whole-grain roll – or as the basis of a nourishing stew or a piquant sauce.

VEGETABLE STOCK

Ingredients

3 large carrots, scrubbed but not peeled, coarsely chopped
1 turnip, coarsely chopped
2 onions, coarsely chopped
2 leeks, coarsely chopped
4 ribs celery, including tops, coarsely chopped
coarsely chopped trimmings from cauliflower, spinach, broccoli or any other vegetables, so long as they are fresh and clean. Always use fresh vegetables.
150 g any dried beans, having been soaked overnight, if necessary; or use rice or barley
2 Tbsp olive oil
1 bouquet garni, which includes 3 sprigs parsley, 1 sprig thyme and 1 bay leaf
1 Tbsp peppercorns
Approx 3.6 litres cold water for 1 kg vegetables

Method

Warm the olive oil in a stockpot, add the vegetables and simmer, stirring continuously for 15 minutes until they start to colour slightly. Then add the water and the other ingredients and bring to simmering point. Simmer for at least 2 hours, adding more water if necessary. Then strain through cheesecloth or use a non-metallic colander. Use or freeze, as required.

CHICKEN STOCK

Ingredients

The bones of a chicken, and, if available, a ham bone or a veal knuckle (ask your butcher for one)
2 leeks, coarsely chopped
2 large carrots, scrubbed but not peeled, coarsely chopped
3 large onions, coarsely chopped
2 ribs celery, tops included, coarsely chopped
6 sprigs parsley, coarsely chopped
1 large clove garlic
2 cloves
1 Tbsp peppercorns
Lemon rind from half a lemon

Method

Place the bones in a stockpot and cover with cold water. Bring to simmering point – do not allow to boil. Simmer for at least an hour, then add all other ingredients and more cold water to cover, if necessary. Return to simmering point and simmer for another 2 hours. Then strain through muslin or use a non-metallic colander. Refrigerate, and when stock has set remove any fat from the top. Use or freeze, as required.

FISH STOCK

Ingredients

1 kg fish bones, heads (with gills removed) and tails (sole or plaice are tastiest, but any other white, non-only fish will do)
1 large onion, coarsely chopped
2 shallots, coarsely chopped
2 ribs celery, tops included, coarsely chopped
2 large carrots, scrubbed but not peeled, coarsely chopped
2 bay leaves
2 cloves
6 sprigs of parsley, coarsely chopped
1 Tbsp peppercorns
Lemon rind from half a lemon
Cold water to cover

Method

Place everything in a stockpot and bring to simmering point – do not allow to boil. Simmer for 20–30 minutes, but no longer or the stock will become bitter. Strain through muslin or use a non-metallic colander. Reduce the strained stock by boiling, if required. Use or freeze, as required.

Seafood is very high in proteins, but does not need to cook for as long as meat.

A HEALTHY LIFESTYLE

Eating a healthy diet is only one part of a healthy lifestyle. To reduce the risk of developing cancer and high blood pressure, to lower cholesterol levels, promote cardiovascular health and improve the quality of your life, you should also:

- **Give up smoking** – if you smoke, you are massively increasing the risk that you will develop lung, mouth, or throat cancer, and more than doubling the risk of having a heart attack, as well as lessening your chances of surviving a heart attack

- **Manage stress** – use relaxation techniques and anger-management methods to cope with stress and keep your blood pressure low

- **Lose weight** – if you are overweight, you are more at risk of developing certain cancers and between two and six times more likely to develop high blood pressure

- **Cut down on alcohol** – there's evidence to suggest that two units of alcohol, and especially of red wine, can reduce blood pressure, but more than this can increase the risk of certain cancers and actually raise blood pressure

- **Lead an active life** – even small amounts of physical activity, for example walking or gardening, can increase the number of calories that you burn and so help lose weight, as well as reducing the risk of developing cancers and heart disease.

Eating nutritiously is important, as well as getting plenty of exercise. Stick to low-fat foods and plenty of fruit and vegetables.

TABLES

These tables give the nutritional values for the main ingredients used in the recipes that follow. To eat healthily and minimise your risk of developing cancer, the major part of your diet should consist of foods with a high fibre content, a low fat content, moderate protein levels, a low or medium carbohydrate (glycaemic index) value and with plenty of antioxidants. Use the Healthy Eating Pyramid on page 21 as a guide to proportions.

Remember that carrying excess weight is a major risk for developing ill health, and watch your calorie intake, too. Doctors recommend that men with a sedentary lifestyle – that of an office worker, say – should eat 2,700 calories a day, while women should eat 2,000. In order to lose weight gradually, at the rate of a pound a week, you need to reduce this figure by 500 calories.

Food	Quantity	Carbohydrate	Fat	Protein	Fibre	Calories
Meat and Dairy						
Cheese, feta	20 g	M	6	4	0	80
Cheese, hard	20 g	H	9.4	7	0	115
Chicken skinless	100 g	L	5	30	0	150
Crème fraîche, regular	100 g	H	50	3	0	440
Egg	1 medium	M	5.5	6	0	80
lean beef, lamb, pork	100 g	M	7	30	0	190
Milk, full fat	250 ml	L	10	8	0	170
Rabbit	100 g	L	4.5	30	0	160
Wild fowl	100 g	L	6	30	0	155
Yoghurt	100 g	L	0	5	0	40
Fish						
Herring, salmon	100 g	L	11	20	0	180
Lobster	250 g	L	1.5	32	0	160
Mackerel	100 g	L	18	25	0	220
Prawn	100 g	L	1	32	0	100
Sardine	100 g	L	2	15	0	65
Scallop	250 g	L	2.5	32	0	165
Shellfish	100 g	L	1	15	0	105
Trout	100 g	L	6	20	0	155
Tuna	100 g	L	3	20	0	120
White fish	100 g	L	2	20	0	90

Prawns are an excellent low-calorie choice, and they are a rich source of protein, vitamins and minerals.

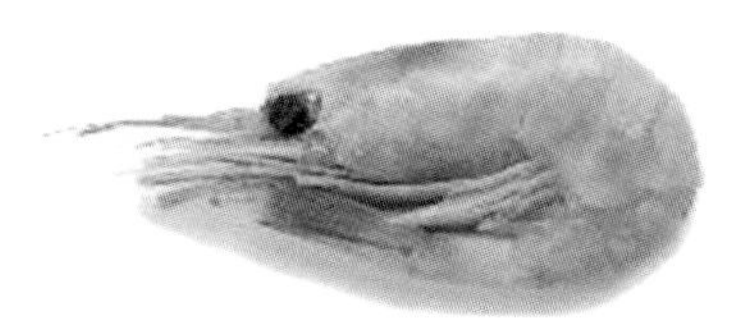

Food	Quantity	Carbohydrate	Fat	Protein	Fibre	Calories
Fruit						
Apple	1 medium	L	0	0.5	2	45
Apricot	3	M	0	1.5	2	30
Banana	1 small	M	0.5	1	1	90
Berries, fresh	100 g	L	0	0.5	1	30
Dried fruit	50 g	M	0	0.5	4	80
Grapefruit	half	L	0	0.5	1	30
Melon	slice	M	0	0.5	1	50
Nectarine, peach	1 medium	L	0	0.5	1	35
Orange	1 medium	L	0	1.5	3	50
Vegetables						
Avocado	$^1/_2$ medium	L	15	2	3.5	150
Beetroot	small	L	0	0.5	0.5	25
Broccoli	100 g	L	0	1.5	2.5	25
Cabbage	50 g	L	0	1	1	7
Carrot	50 g	L	0	0.5	1	12
Aubergine	100 g	L	0	0.5	2	75

Fruit is easily digested and has many health benefits.

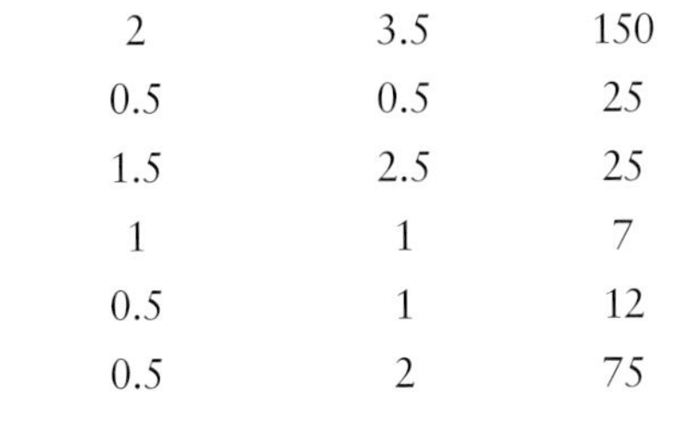

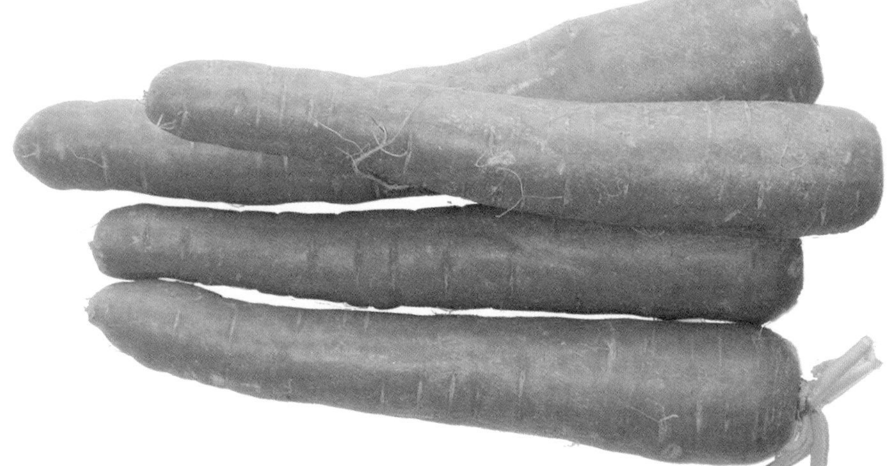

Carrots are high in beta-carotene (providing vitamin A value) and cooking carrots actually enhances the digestibility of the beta-carotene.

Food	Quantity	Carbohydrate	Fat	Protein	Fibre	Calories
Vegetables *(continued)*						
Cauliflower	100 g	L	0	1	1.5	20
Cucumber	60 g	L	0	0.2	0.5	4
Green beans	100 g	L	0	1.5	2.5	20
Leek	60 g	L	0	0.5	0.8	9
Lettuce	40 g	L	0	0.5	0.3	5
Onions	medium	L	0	1	1.4	30
Peas	100 g	L	0	3.5	6	60
Peppers	100 g	L	0	1	2.5	30
Soyabean	100 g	L	7	8	6	120
Spinach	50 g cooked	L	0	1	1	10
Sweetcorn	100 g	M	0.5	2.5	1.5	95
Tofu	100 g	L	4	8	0	70
Tomato	medium	L	0	1	1	15

Eating raw onions can help to increase your high-density lipoprotein cholesterol (HDL) levels. This good type of cholesterol can help to keep blood pressure low, so reducing the risk of cardiovascular disease and stroke.

Peppers are low in calories and are especially rich in vitamins A and C. Surprisingly, a pepper contains three to four times more vitamin C than an orange. They do not contain any fat.

Food	Quantity	Carbohydrate	Fat	Protein	Fibre	Calories
Cereal, Nuts, Pulses						
Barley	50 g raw	L	1	2	1	140
Buckwheat	100 g	L	2.5	3	2.1	330
Chickpeas	100 g	L	3	5	4	110
Cornstarch	100 g	M	0.7	2	0.1	350
Lentils	100 g	L	0.5	8	2	100
Oats	50 g raw	L	1	4	3	140
Pasta, wholegrain	100 g	L	1	5	4	120
Rice, brown, basmati	100 g	M	0	3.5	1	200
Walnuts	2 tbsp	L	8	2	1	80
Wild rice	100 g	M	0	3	1	100

BREAKFASTS

WILD MUSHROOM OMELETTE

SERVES **4**

This delicious mixture of eggs and mushrooms is full of protein and vitamins, and ensures a good start to the day.

450 g chanterelle mushrooms
6 fresh eggs
1 tbsp fresh herbs, chopped
salt substitute (see page 14) and freshly ground black pepper
3 tbsp olive oil

1. Beat the eggs with the herbs and salt substitute and pepper. Slice the chanterelles.
2. Put the olive oil in a non-stick frying pan or pan. Cook the chanterelles for about five minutes, then add the egg mixture. Cook over a moderate heat until almost set. Fold and serve immediately.

NUTRITIONAL VALUES

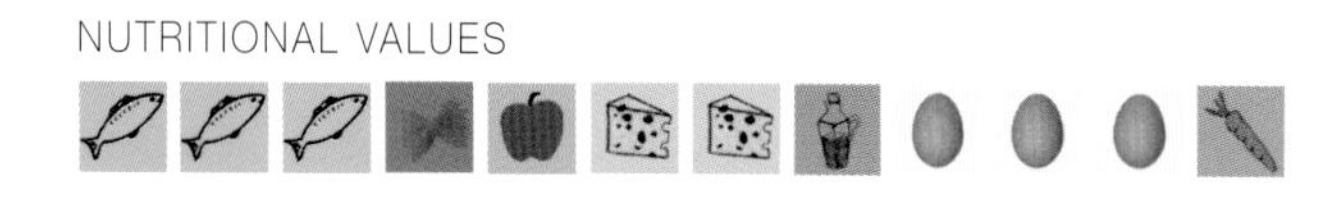

HAM 'N' EGG COCOTTES

SERVES **4**

These popular favourites are perfect as an appetizer or for a special breakfast or brunch.

40 g ham, cut into strips

60 g stick butter

225 g cups button mushrooms, wiped and sliced

freshly ground ground black pepper

4 medium eggs

4 tbsp low-fat heavy cream

200 g cup Brie, cubed

1 Preheat the oven to 190°C/gas mark 5 for 10 minutes prior to baking the cocottes. Line four ramekin dishes with the ham. Melt the butter in a small frying pan and gently sauté the mushrooms for 2 minutes. Drain on paper towels and place in the ramekin dishes. Season with black pepper.

2 Break an egg into each dish, then pour over 1 tablespoon low-fat cream. Dot with the cheese. Place in a roasting tin half-filled with boiling water (bain marie), then bake for 15–20 minutes or until set, as liked.

NUTRITIONAL VALUES

OMELETTE FINES HERBES

SERVES **1**

Packed with nutrients, this omelette is a classic French dish.

2 medium eggs

salt substitute (see page 14) and freshly ground black pepper

1 tbsp chopped herbs (try parsley, chervil, tarragon and chives)

1 tbsp water

1 tbsp olive oil

1 Lightly whisk the eggs with the seasoning to taste until frothy. Stir in the herbs and water.

2 Heat the oil in a frying pan, tilting the frying pan to coat the base evenly. Pour in the beaten eggs; stir gently with a fork, drawing the mixture form the sides of the frying pan to the centre. When the egg has set, stop stirring, and cook for a further minute. Then, with a palette knife, fold over a third of the omelette to the centre, then fold over the opposite side.

3 To serve, gently slide the omelette onto a warmed plate and serve immediately.

IDEAS FOR ALTERNATIVE FILLINGS

Try stirring 65 g grated cheese into the eggs when the base has set, or 90 g mushrooms, sliced and sautéed.

Place mushrooms, ham, tomatoes, and prawns in the centre of the omelette once set. Cook for 1 to 2 minutes to heat through. Fold over and serve immediately, sprinkled with parsley, chopped fine.

NUTRITIONAL VALUES

PIPÉRADE

SERVES **2–3**

This is a Mediterranean version of scrambled eggs.

- 2 tbsp olive oil
- 1 onion, chopped
- 2 cloves garlic, crushed
- 1 red, 1 yellow and 1 green pepper, seeded and sliced
- 6 medium eggs
- salt substitute (see page 14) and freshly ground black pepper
- 2 tbsp water
- 3 tomatoes, chopped
- 2 tbsp basil, chopped

1. Heat the oil in a large frying pan and sauté the onion, garlic, and peppers for 10 minutes until soft.
2. Beat the eggs with the seasoning and 2 tablespoons water, and add to the frying pan with the tomatoes. Cook, stirring, until almost set.
3. Sprinkle over the basil.

NUTRITIONAL VALUES

KHAGINA

SERVES **2**

Khagina is a light, spicy egg dish, which can be made in various ways.

50 g onion, thinly sliced
2 green chillies, chopped
1 tbsp olive oil
25 g red pepper, cut into juliennes
2 cloves garlic
pinch of chilli powder
pinch of salt substitute (see page 14)
2 medium eggs
freshly ground black pepper
2 tbsp chives, chopped

1 Sweat the onion and green chillies in the oil in a non-stick frying pan over a low heat for 4–5 minutes, adding a tiny amount of water between stirs to keep them from sticking and burning.

2 Add the red pepper and garlic and cook for 3–4 minutes, stirring continuously.

3 Add the chilli powder, salt substitute, and 2 tablespoons of water and let it simmer again for 2–3 minutes.

4 Break the eggs gently on top of the bed of vegetables and spices in the pan, taking care to keep the egg yolks intact. Shake the pan so that the egg white spreads to fill the pan. Do not overcook the egg yolks – they are done when, if you were to pierce them with a fork, they would ooze out and run slightly.

5 Grind black pepper over the top, then sprinkle the chives over and serve immediately.

NUTRITIONAL VALUES

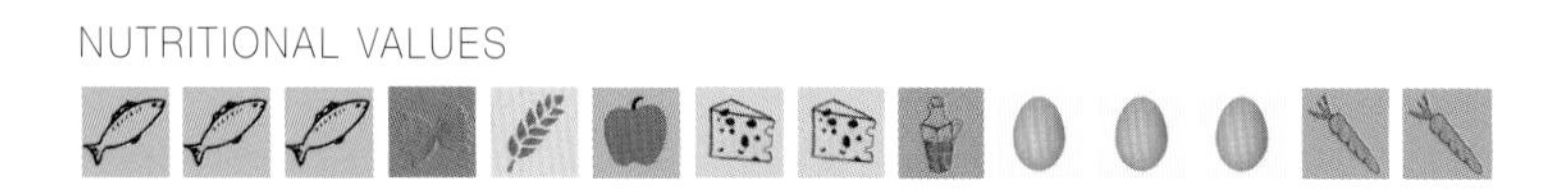

LIGHT MEALS

SALADE TIEDE

SERVES **4**

Warm salad of sautéed mushrooms, goat's cheese and asparagus. This is quintessential bistro fare. You could, if you liked, add a handful of grated prosciutto and/or toasted hazelnuts to this simply prepared but delicious salad.

350 g small thin asparagus, tough ends broken off
3 shallots, chopped
2 cloves garlic, chopped
4 tbsp olive oil
200 g mixed salad greens
freshly ground black pepper, to taste
1 tbsp tarragon mustard
1 tbsp raspberry or red wine vinegar
100 g low-fat goat's cheese, crumbled or broken into small pieces
350 g mixed fresh mushrooms, such as oyster, chanterelles, enaki, porcini, and button, cut into strips or bite-size pieces
1 tbsp balsamic vinegar or red wine
½ tbsp chopped fresh chervil or parsley
2 tbsp fresh chives, snipped, or fresh tarragon, chopped

1. Cook the asparagus in rapidly boiling water until just tender and bright green, about 3 minutes. Drain, submerge in very cold water (add a few ice cubes to the water) to keep its bright green colour and crisp texture, then drain once again. Set the asparagus aside while you prepare the rest of the salad.

2. Mix 1 tablespoon of the chopped shallots with half the garlic and 1–2 tablespoon olive oil. Toss this with the greens, along with pepper to taste.

3. Mix 1 tablespoon olive oil with the tarragon mustard and the raspberry or red wine vinegar, stir well then pour over the greens and toss well. Arrange asparagus and low-fat goat's cheese over the top.

4. Sauté the mushrooms over a medium–high heat, with the remaining shallots and garlic, in the remaining olive oil until lightly browned. Pour in the balsamic vinegar. Serve immediately, with the herbs scattered over.

NUTRITIONAL VALUES

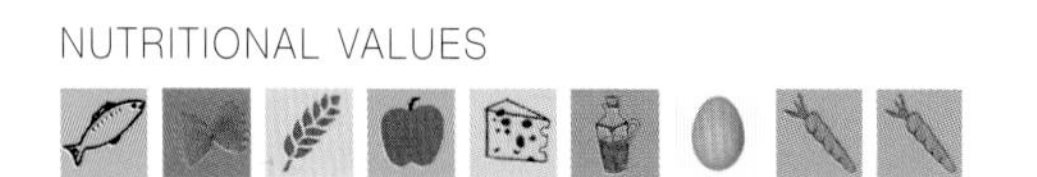

BLACKENED TUNA WITH STRAWBERRIES

SERVES **2**

An unusual but wonderful combination that tastes great and looks colourful.

60 g unsalted butter
5–6 large strawberries, hulled and cut into thirds
1/2 tsp ground cumin
1/2 tsp ground cinnamon
1/2 tsp ground marjoram
1/2 tsp cayenne pepper
1/2 tsp freshly ground black pepper
2 x 250 g tuna steaks
4 tbsp groundnut oil

1. In a small frying pan over a low heat, melt the butter and add the strawberries. Sauté the strawberries for 3 minutes, until soft. Set aside.
2. Mix together the cumin, cinnamon, marjoram, cayenne pepper and black pepper. Season the tuna generously with the mixture.
3. In a small cast-iron frying pan, heat the groundnut oil over a high heat. Sear the fish until black, about 3–4 minutes. Turn over and blacken the other side, another 2–3 minutes. (This will produce a lot of smoke.)
4. Garnish the tuna with the strawberries and serve.

NUTRITIONAL VALUES

GRILLED SCALLOP KEBABS

SERVES **2–4**

Rice vinegar begins to 'cook' the scallops in the same way that lime juice 'cooks' fish when making Mexican ceviche, so the scallops need only brief cooking under the grill if they are not to become overcooked.

12 large scallops
1 clove garlic, crushed and finely chopped
1 tbsp spring onion, green part, finely chopped
2 tbsp soy sauce
2 tsp rice vinegar
1 tbsp sesame oil
1 cm crushed tomato sesame seeds
pinch of chilli powder

1. Cut each scallop in half horizontally. Thread the scallops on to skewers and lay them in a shallow, non-metallic dish.
2. Mix together the remaining ingredients and pour over the scallops. Turn the skewers over and leave for 15–20 minutes, turning occasionally.
3. Preheat the grill.
4. Lift the skewers from the marinade and cook under the grill for about 4 minutes, turning occasionally and brushing with the marinade.

NUTRITIONAL VALUES

POACHED SALMON

SERVES **8–10**

This is a dish that is often served cold; but it can be served hot with Hollandaise or Mousseline sauce.

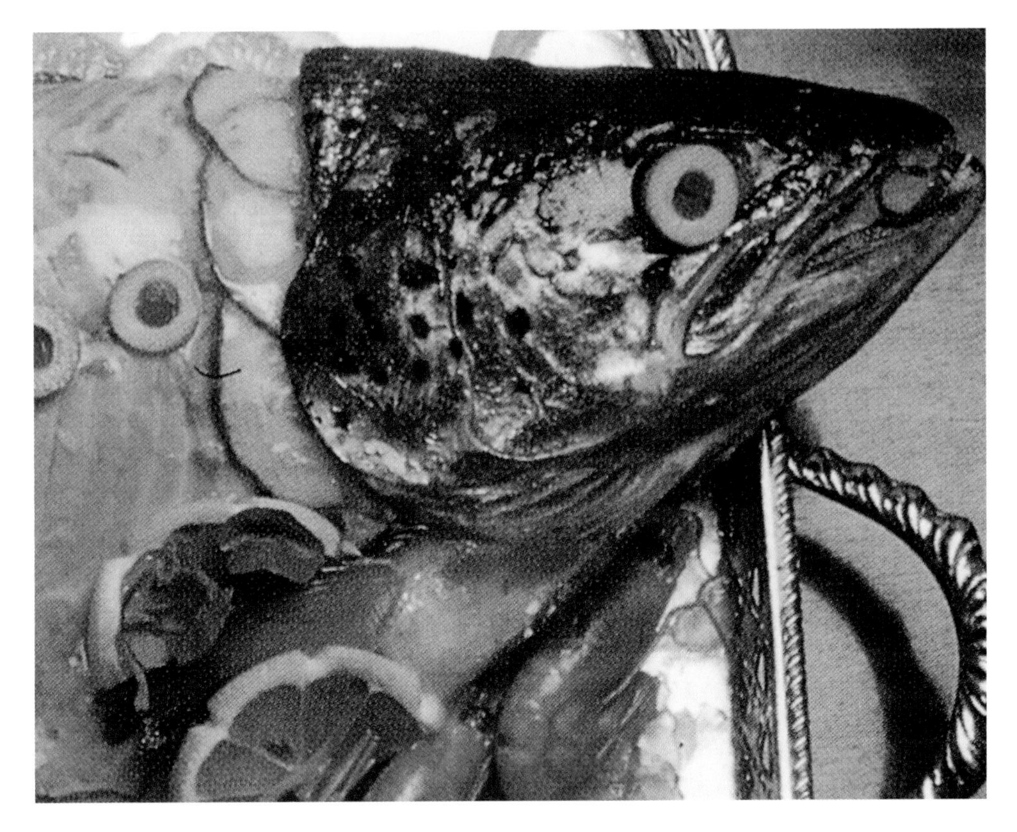

4 kg salmon
½ lemon
½ onion
1 bay leaf
1 sprig parsley
court-bouillon

1 Prepare the salmon by slitting the stomach and removing the insides from head to tail. Wash the cavity under cold running water.

2 Place half a lemon, 2 small pieces of onion, a bay leaf and sprig of parsley in the cavity. (The fish can be gutted by removing the head and drawing the entrails out with the curved handle of a soup ladle. This means the stomach remains whole and is better to dress for a buffet table. However many fish are bought already gutted.)

3 Half fill a fish kettle with the court-bouillon and lower the fish into the cold liquid, bring to the boil gently and then simmer over a low heat for about 45 minutes. Remove from the heat and allow to cool for some hours in the fish liquid. (Note: do not cook over a high heat or the fish will split.)

4 Remove fish from the liquid and allow to drain for about 1 hour if using cold, as a dressed salmon. Alternatively serve the salmon hot with Hollandaise or Mousseline Sauce.

NUTRITIONAL VALUES

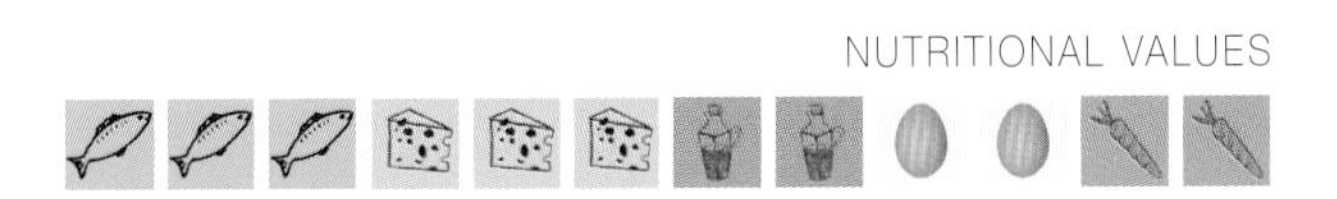

LOBSTER AND CHICKEN BROCHETTES

SERVES **4**

These brochettes are served with garlic and tomato mayonnaise and lime wedges alonside a crisp green salad.

2 fresh lobsters, each 750 g

2 chicken breasts, each 250 g, cubed into bite-size pieces

125 ml dry white wine

125 ml garlic and tomato mayonnaise

GARLIC AND TOMATO MAYONNAISE

To 300 ml cups mayonnaise add half its volume plum tomatoes, canned, and mix in a food processor, adding pepper, and plenty of garlic – 2 tsp for every 300 ml cups mayonnaise

Lime wedges, to serve

1. Place the lobsters in a pot of boiling salted water. Lower heat and simmer for 5minutes, or until they go pink. Remove from pot and allow to cool before handling.
2. Pull the tail section away from the head with a little twist. Remove the shells and cut the flesh into bite-size chunks.
3. Poach the chicken pieces in the white wine for 6–8 minutes. Cool.
4. Arrange the lobster and chicken alternatively on the skewers.
5. Serve with the garlic and tomato mayonnaise and lime wedges.

NUTRITIONAL VALUES

SPICY MONKFISH BROCHETTES

SERVES **4**

For this delicious, colourful recipe, you will need six large skewers.

1 kg monkfish tail
250 ml water
125 ml lime juice

FOR THE SAUCE

4 red chillies, deseeded and chopped
olive oil
2 large tomatoes, peeled and chopped
1 tsp dried oregano
1 tsp freshly ground black pepper
1 tsp cumin seed
1 tsp ground ginger
2 tsp garlic
625 ml fish stock
1/2 large cucumber
1 medium red onion
Lime wedges, to serve
tabasco sauce, to taste

1 Skin, bone and cube the fish. Marinate in the water and lime juice for four hours, or overnight if possible.

2 Fry the chilli in a little olive oil, until dark. Add the chopped tomato, oregano, black pepper, cumin seed, ginger, garlic and fish stock to the chillies. Bring to the boil and simmer for 10 minutes. Remove from the heat.

3 Cut the cucumber into 6 mm rounds. Cut the red onion into eighths, by halving like an orange, then quartering each half.

4 Make up the skewers, by piercing a piece of onion, a piece of fish, a piece of cucumber, etc., until the skewer is full. Coat the full skewer liberally with the sauce.

5 Serve with lime wedges and tabasco sauce.

NUTRITIONAL VALUES

LOBSTER WITH BUTTER SAUCE

SERVES **4**

The tangy sauce complements the delicate flavour of the lobster tails exceptionally well. Whole, cooked and halved lobsters are good served this way too.

4 uncooked lobster tails

FOR THE SAUCE

4 tbsp butter

4 tbsp lemon juice

1 tbsp finely grated lemon rind

4 tbsp snipped fresh chives

2 tbsp chopped fresh tarragon

1. Place the lobster tails in a shallow dish.

2. To make the sauce, put the butter into a small pan and add the lemon juice and lemon rind. Heat gently until melted, then stir in the herbs.

3. Brush the butter sauce generously over the lobster tails then transfer them to the barbecue. Cook over a medium–high heat for about 8–10 minutes, turning occasionally and brushing with more sauce, until the lobster is just opaque.

4. Reheat any remaining butter sauce and serve separately.

5. Serve with a green salad.

NUTRITIONAL VALUES

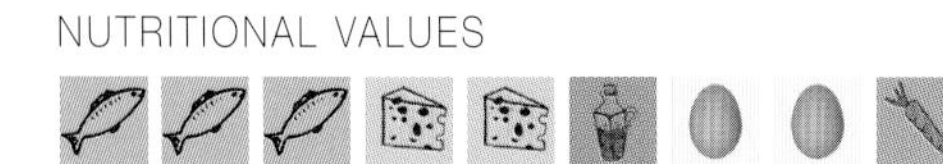

SLOW COOKED SALMON WITH ASIAN GREENS

SERVES **4**

This recipe was originally created at the Ritz-Carlton Hotel, Millenia, Singapore. It has been changed slightly to make it easier for home cooking, but the salmon should melt in the mouth just the same as the original.

300 g baby bok choy, whole
4 x 225 g salmon fillets, grey parts removed
3 tbsp olive oil
salt substitute (see page 14) and freshly ground black pepper
2.5 cm piece root ginger, peeled and juilienned
450 ml vegetable (see page 23) or fish stock (see page 24)
300 g bamboo shoots, julienned
300 g shiitake mushrooms, stems removed, halved or quartered
120 g spring onions, julienned

NUTRITIONAL VALUES

1. Preheat the oven to a low heat – ideally 110°C/gas mark 1/4. (Note: if your oven doesn't have a setting of gas mark 1/4, you will need to meaure the temperature with a special oven thermometer, which are available to buy in many shops.)
2. Blanch the baby bok choy by covering it in boiling water for 30 seconds, then plunging it in icy water. Drain and cut it in half lengthways, then set it aside.
3. On the lowest rack of the oven, place an uncovered, ovenproof pan of hot water. The evaporating water will help to keep the fish moist while cooking. Lightly brush the salmon with the oil and season with pepper. Bake an ovenproof dish for 40–50 minutes, depending on how well-cooked you prefer your salmon.
4. In another pan, place the root ginger and stock, bring to the boil, add the bok choy, bamboo shoots, and mushrooms. Turn the heat down to a simmer and cook for 10 minutes.
5. Ladle some stock and vegetables into a bowl making sure the root ginger remains in the pan. Place a piece of salmon over the vegetables and garnish with the cooked root ginger and the spring onions.

GREEN PAPAYA SEAFOOD SALAD WITH CITRUS SOY DRESSING

SERVES **2–4**

Many seafood salads are laden with mayonnaise but seafood is best when combined with a tart partner, so here green papaya, with its naturally sour taste, is used as a perfect complement to the prawns, crab and calamari.

10 large prawns, uncooked, with shells
120 g uncooked calamari
120 g cooked crabmeat
1 medium green papaya, grated or julienned
1 tbsp coriander or parsley leaves, chopped, to garnish

FOR THE DRESSING

2 cloves garlic, crushed
4 tbsp light soy sauce
1 tbsp lemon juice
1 tbsp lime juice

1. Blanch the prawns and calamari by covering them with boiling water. Remove the calamari after 2 minutes or it will become tough, but leave the prawns for 2 minutes more. Then plunge both into icy water.

2. When chilled, peel and devein the prawns and cut halfway across the body lengthways and halfway across widthways. Cut the calamari into small pieces equal to the size of the prawns. Mix together the prawns, calamari and cooked crabmeat.

3. Arrange the papaya strips loosely and place the seafood around them.

4. In a jar or bowl mix together the ingredients for the dressing. Drizzle the dressing on to the papaya and seafood, sprinkle with chopped coriander and serve.

NUTRITIONAL VALUES

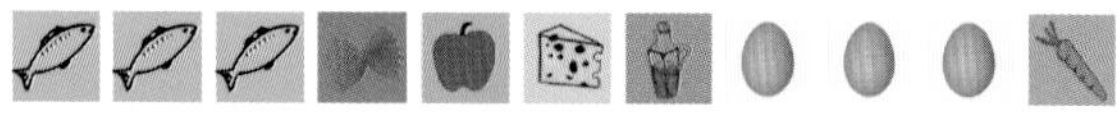

SOLE WITH SNOW PEAS

SERVES **4**

This makes a beautifully colourful light meal, or can be served in smaller potions as a starter.

75 g snow peas

2 small carrots, julienned

freshly ground white pepper

8 fillets of sole, cut in half lengthways

2 tsp olive oil

peel of 2 oranges, cut into short julienne

1 tbsp very finely chopped ginger-root

2 tbsp soy sauce

7 tbsp fine sherry

a squeeze of lemon juice

4 tbsp water

NUTRITIONAL VALUES

1 Arrange the snow peas and carrots in a large steamer or 2 small ones. Sprinkle with freshly ground white pepper. Season the skin side of the pieces of sole, then roll them up loosely, seasoned side innermost, starting from the narrow end. Place a little way apart on the vegetables. Place a piece of ginger on each piece of fish.

2 Place the steamer over a pan of simmering water and steam for about 8 minutes until the sole is just opaque all the way through.

3 Meanwhile, heat the oil. Add the orange julienne and cook until just beginning to curl. Stir in the chopped ginger and cook for about 30 seconds, then stir in the soy sauce, sherry, lemon juice, and water. Bring to the boil, then reduce the heat and simmer for 5 minutes.

4 Spoon the sauce onto parts of 4 warmed plates. Carefully place the rolls of sole on the sauce. Scatter the orange julienne on the rolls and garnish the plates with the vegetables.

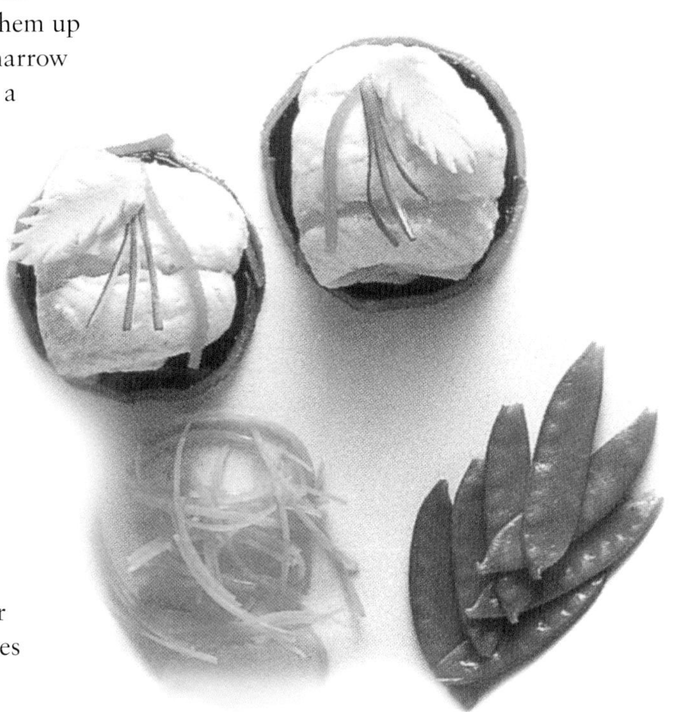

GOUJONS OF BRILL WITH RED CURRANT DRESSING

SERVES **4**

A lovely, light and fruity meal, ideal on a warm sunny day.

4 fillets of brill, each approximately 175 g, skinned and cut into strips
oak leaf lettuce

FOR THE DRESSING

3 tbsp champagne vinegar
150 ml olive oil
3 tbsp red current juice
1½ tbsp finely snipped chives
200 g red currants
freshly ground black pepper

FOR THE GARNISH

red currants
sprigs of chervil

1. Shake all the ingredients for the dressing together.
2. Steam the brill for about 5 minutes until just opaque – take care not to overcook. Remove the brill from the heat, cover, and keep warm.
3. Gently warm the dressing. Meanwhile, arrange the lettuce on 4 large chilled plates.
4. Arrange the brill in the centre of the plates and spoon the dressing over. Garnish with red currants and sprigs of chervil.

NUTRITIONAL VALUES

PANACHE OF SEAFOOD

SERVES **4**

Start to cook the seabass and monkfish before adding the John Dory and then the scallops to the steamer – the more delicate fish will become too tough if cooked for the same length of time as the firmer ones.

125 g skinned, boned salmon
1/2 tsp egg white
80 ml low-fat double cream, chilled
cayenne pepper
a few strands of saffron
250 ml fish stock (see page 24)
125 ml dry white wine
1 1/2 tsp lemon juice
freshly ground white pepper
4 scallops
350 g John Dory fillets
225 g sea bass fillets
225 g monkfish fillets

FOR THE GARNISH

sprigs of coriander and chervil

1. Purée the salmon in a food processor or blender. Add the egg white. Pass through a strainer into a bowl over a bowl of ice, then gradually beat in the chilled cream. Add a little cayenne pepper, cover, and chill for 30 minutes.

2. Pipe the salmon mixture into 4 small decorative moulds, pushing it well into the sides. Place the moulds in a shallow pan, surround with hot water, place over a low heat and poached for 10 minutes. Leave to stand off the heat for 2 minutes.

3. Stir the saffron into a little of the stock. Bring the remaining stock, wine, and lemon juice to the boil and reduce by three-quarters. Stir in the low-fat cream and saffron liquid and simmer for 2 minutes. Season and add a little more lemon juice if needed.

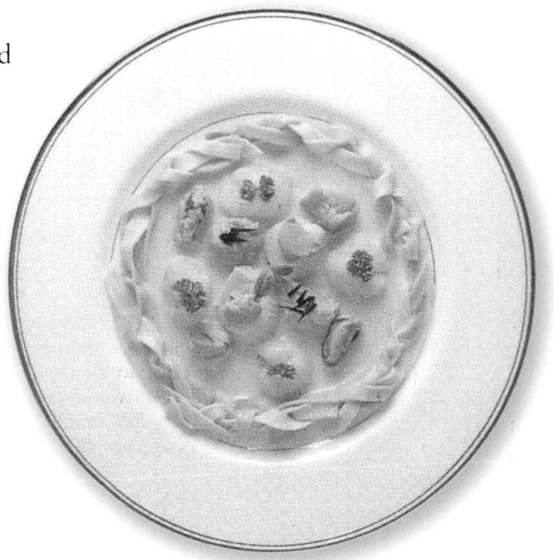

4. Open the scallops and cut the other fish into 4 pieces each. Season the fish and steam for 3–5 minutes until just opaque.

5. Unmould the salmon onto 4 plates. Spoon the sauce around and place the fish on top. Garnish with coriander and chervil.

NUTRITIONAL VALUES

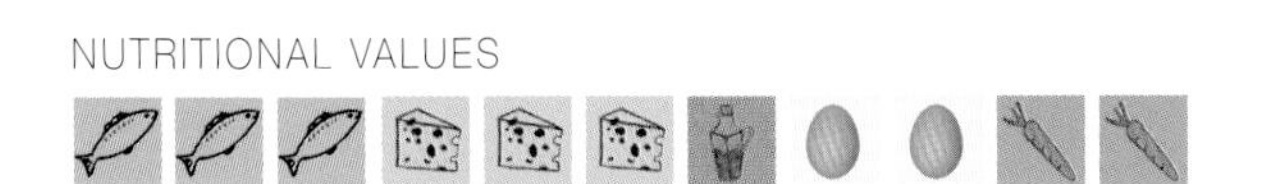

GARLIC PRAWNS WITH BAKED EGGS

SERVES **4**

This is such an easy dish to make but looks very appetizing.

6 cloves garlic, chopped
2 tbsp olive oil
250 g shelled prawns
4 eggs

1. Fry the garlic in the oil, stirring, until lightly browned.
2. Add the prawns and stir-fry until coated with garlic and oil.
3. Divide the mixture between 4 lightly oiled individual serving dishes. Break an egg to one side of each dish. Cover the dishes with foil and cook in a moderate oven for 3–4 minutes, until the whites are just set.

NUTRITIONAL VALUES

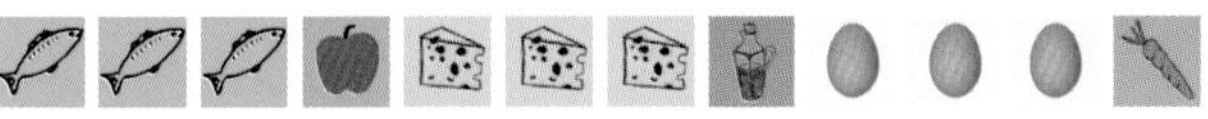

CARNE CON CHILE COLORADO

SERVES **4**

Rather than being a mixture of cheap minced beef, beans, and tomato sauce, this recipe consists of large chunks of tender meat in a thick, smooth, rich sauce.

8 middle-sized dried chillies: California or New Mexico type, deseeded and deveined
1/2 tsp cumin seeds
3 cloves garlic, peeled
1 small onion, chopped
1 tsp dried oregano
700 g lean, boneless beef or pork
oil for frying
450 ml water or stock (see pages 23-4)
salt substitute (see page 14) to taste

1. Tear the chillies into reasonably flat pieces, then toast them briefly in a hot, dry frying pan. Hold them down for a few seconds until they change colour and crackle. Repeat on the other side. Do not allow them to burn or they will become bitter. Transfer them to a bowl and cover with boiling water. Place a saucer on top to keep them submerged and leave to soak for at least 30 minutes. While they are soaking, grind the cumin seeds in a pestle and mortar or spice grinder.

2. Drain the chillies, but keep 225 ml of the soaking liquid. Add the garlic, onion, oregano and fresh-ground cumin. Purée the lot, with the soaking liquid, in a blender. Blend until smooth, then strain through a wire sieve: this is one of the most time-consuming parts, but it makes for a wonderfully smooth sauce.

3. Cut the meat into approximately 2.5 cm cubes, and fry in a heavy, deep frying pan with a little oil until browned all over – about 10 minutes. Keep turning the meat and scraping the pan.

4. Add the strained sauce; continue to cook, stirring and scraping frequently to avoid burning, for a few minutes (5 at most). The purée should be thick and rather darker than when you started. Add the water or stock; bring to the boil, and simmer over a low heat for at least an hour, stirring occasionally. If the sauce gets too thick, add a little more water or stock. It is ready when the meat is very tender. Serve with a green salad.

NUTRITIONAL VALUES

SAUTÉED MIXED MUSHROOMS WITH BACON

SERVES **4**

This bistro-style dish is simple to prepare and marvellous for a winter supper. Any firm fleshy flavourful mushroom is fine; oyster mushrooms, chanterelles, trompette de la mort, and perhaps a few slices of porcini.

450–675 g mixed fresh mushrooms, cut into bite-size pieces
40–50 g butter, or half butter and half olive oil
1 shallot, chopped
175 g smoked bacon or good ham, such as prosciutto or jamon, cut into bite-size pieces
1 clove garlic, chopped
a handful of watercress or mâche, roughly chopped
1 tbsp chopped fresh chervil, tarragon, parsley, or a combination

NUTRITIONAL VALUES

1 Lightly sauté the mushrooms in the butter, or butter and olive oil, with the shallot and bacon or ham. When the mushrooms and bacon are browned, stir in the garlic and cook for a few moments more.

2 Serve garnished with the tufts of watercress or mâche, which will wilt slightly, and chopped herbs.

CHICKEN LIVERS WITH SHERRY VINEGAR

SERVES **4**

This can be served in one large dish, or in smaller individual ones.

500 g chicken livers

1 tsp paprika

1 tsp garlic

1/4 tsp each salt substitute (see page 14) and freshly ground black pepper

60 g stick butter, melted

1/2 onion, finely chopped

60 ml sherry vinegar

300 ml chicken stock (see page 24)

60 g butter

1. Wash and trim the chicken livers to remove the green bile sacs and any gristle.

2. Mix the paprika, garlic, salt and pepper together in a bowl. Toss the livers to cover in the mix.

3. Heat the 60 g of melted butter in a large frying pan. Cook the livers over high heat in the butter, stirring continuously, until sealed and browned all over. Place livers in a warmed bowl.

4. Add the onion to the pan and soften over a lower heat. Turn up the heat again, add the vinegar and sugar, and cook until the vinegar is almost dry. Add the stock, stir and reduce to half the quantity.

5. Take the remaining 60 g butter, break into small pieces, and stir until it melts into the liquid. Check the seasoning and pour the sauce over the livers and serve.

NUTRITIONAL VALUES

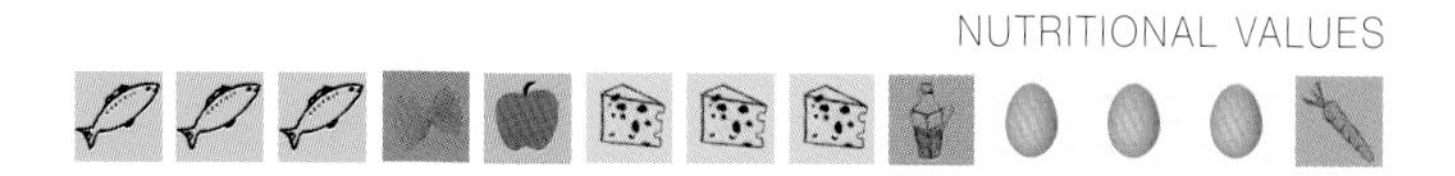

SMOKED CHICKEN, BACON AND PRAWN SALAD

SERVES **4 – 5**

This salad makes the perfect starter, as it can be prepared well in advance and assembled at the last minute. Alternatively, serve this as a light lunch for two.

175 g smoked chicken breast, cooked

175 g peeled prawns

50 g button mushrooms, thinly sliced

3 rashers lean bacon, derinded

selection of lettuce leaves

DRESSING

6 tbsp olive oil

2 tbsp white wine vinegar

pinch of dry mustard

1 shallot or 1/2 a small, sweet onion, finely chopped

4 tbsp chopped fresh parsley

freshly ground black pepper

GARNISH

fresh chives

1. First make the dressing; combine the first five ingredients in a screw top jar and shake vigorously until well blended. Season with pepper to taste.

2. Slice the chicken breasts into thin strips. Place in a bowl together with the prawns and mushrooms and pour over the dressing. Carefully fold the ingredients together. Cover and chill.

3. Grill the bacon until crisp. Crumble into a bowl.

4. Line four individual serving plates with an assortment of lettuce leaves. Drain the chicken mixture and spoon on top of the salad. Sprinkle with bacon, and garnish with fresh snipped chives.

NUTRITIONAL VALUES

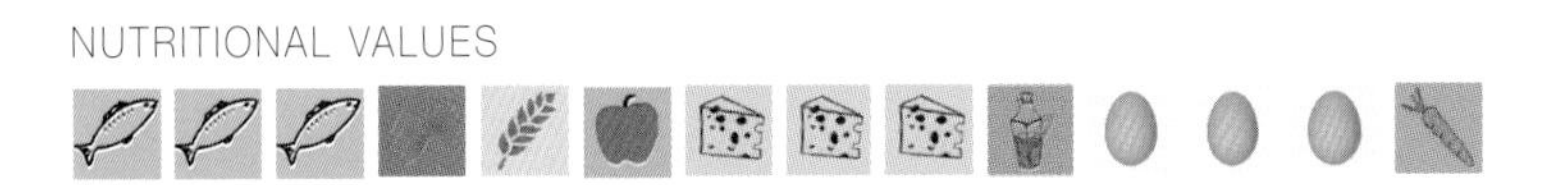

SPICED PORK KEBABS

SERVES **4**

Pinchitos, succulent pork skewers, are especially popular in the Andalusia region of Spain, where families grill them outdoors over an open fire. As with many dishes in Andalusia, Moorish influences abound. Here, they are evidenced in the use of cumin and paprika.

60 ml olive oil

2 cloves garlic, chopped

2 tbsp lemon juice

1 tsp curry powder

1 tsp ground cumin

1 tsp turmeric

1/2 tsp cayenne pepper

1/2 tsp paprika

1/4 tsp thyme

450 g lean pork, cut into small cubes

1 In a shallow dish, combine the olive oil, garlic, lemon juice, curry powder, ground cumin, turmeric, cayenne pepper, paprika and thyme, and mix well. Gently place the pork pieces in the dish and marinate for several hours in the refrigerator. Turn the pork over periodically to ensure that all sides are equally coated.

2 Immediately before grilling, remove the pork pieces from the marinade, and thread them on to skewers. Place the pork skewers on the hot grill, and cook, turning them until the pork is fully cooked on all sides. Serve hot, fresh from the grill.

NUTRITIONAL VALUES

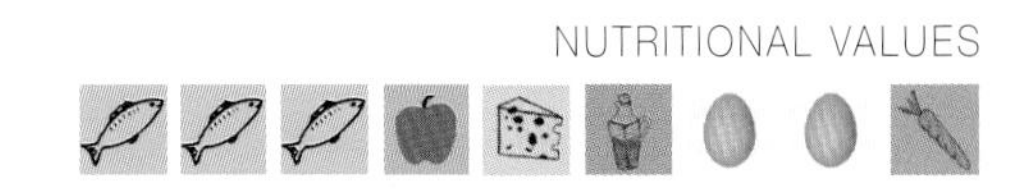

WARM SALAD OF SWEETCORN AND CHICKEN LIVERS

SERVES **4**

A real feast for the eyes, and tastes very good too!

$4^1/_2$ tbsp walnut oil
2 tbsp butter
8 chicken livers
50 g sweetcorn
1 frisée lettuce
1 head of rocket
$4^1/_2$ tbsp vinaigrette
salt substitute (see page 14) and freshly ground black pepper to taste

1 Amalgamate the oil and butter in a frying pan over a high heat. Toss in the chicken livers and sauté for 3 minutes on each side. Add the sweetcorn and remove the pan from the heat.

2 Arrange the frisée and the rocket prettily on each plate and lightly season with the salt substitute and pepper.

3 Add the vinaigrette to the still warm pan and scrape to combine with the pan juices. Dress each salad with two of the chicken livers, pour over half of the pan juices and the sweetcorn, and serve immediately.

NUTRITIONAL VALUES

STARTERS

SEAWEED SOUP

SERVES **6**

A very simple but tasty soup, garnished with sesame seeds and full of goodness.

- 115 g dried wakame, soaked for at least 30 minutes
- 1.5 litres fish (see page 24) or beef stock
- 1 bunch spring onions, white and some green parts chopped
- 1 tbsp sesame oil
- 1 clove garlic, crushed and finely chopped
- 175 g lean tender beef, cut into fine strips
- soy sauce
- toasted sesame seeds for garnish

1. Drain the wakame and cut it into strips.

2. Pour the stock into a saucepan, add the spring onions and bring to the boil. Lower the heat so the stock simmers gently. Heat the oil in a frying pan, add the garlic and beef and stir-fry for about 2 minutes. Add to the stock together with the wakame. Add soy sauce to taste and heat through. Serve garnished with toasted sesame seeds.

NUTRITIONAL VALUES

SPINACH AND MUSSEL POT

SERVES **4**

This is a very tasty way of serving up mussels, garnished with low-fat double cream.

- 450 g spinach
- 1 medium onion, chopped
- 60 g butter
- 1 tsp garlic, crushed
- pinch of nutmeg
- salt substitute (see page 14) and freshly ground black pepper
- 170 ml dry white wine
- 900 ml chicken stock (see page 24)
- 900 g mussels, cleaned
- 2 tbsp low-fat double cream

1. Discard any stalks and large veins if using fresh spinach, and wash thoroughly. (Note: it is only necessary to cook fresh spinach.) Place in boiling water for 2 minutes. Remove and cool under cold water. Squeeze to remove moisture. Finely chop.

2. Fry the onion in the butter. Add the spinach, garlic, nutmeg, salt substitute and black pepper. Stir. Add the white wine and turn up the heat. Cook for 5 minutes, until the wine is almost dry. Add the stock and bring to the boil. Stir and cook for 5 minutes. The consistency should be that of low-fat double cream; if it's too thin, continue cooking over heat, stirring until it thickens.

3. Add the mussels and cover the pot. Cook until the mussels have opened, continuously shaking the pot. Remove from the heat and season to taste. Pour into bowls, evenly distributing the mussels. Swirl a little low-fat cream over each, and serve.

NUTRITIONAL VALUES

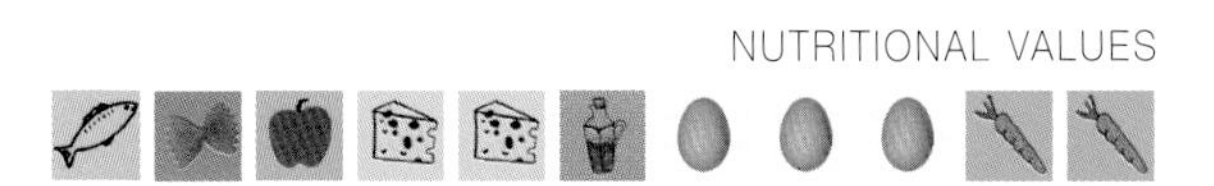

OYSTERS BLOODY MARY

SERVES **4**

These piquant oysters are perfect snacks for parties, and they can also be served as a light starter.

340 ml tomato juice
3 tbsp vodka
5 drops Tabasco sauce
1 tsp Worcestershire sauce
1 tbsp lemon juice
salt substitute (see page 14) and freshly ground black pepper
12 fresh oysters
diced cucumber
small, young celery sticks, diced
lemon wedges, to serve

1 Mix a Bloody Mary using the tomato juice, vodka, Tabasco and Worcestershire sauces, lemon juice and seasoning. Place these ingredients in a blender with some ice cubes so that it is well chilled.

2 Open the oysters carefully. To do this, slide an oyster knife into the back of the shell; sever the hinge close to the flat upper shell. Remove the upper shell and discard.

3 Cut the oyster from the lower shell and pick out any pieces of shell or grit. Place the cleaned oyster in the lower shell.

4 Fill the shells with the Bloody Mary mix and sprinkle cucumber and celery over the top. Serve immediately with lemon wedges.

NUTRITIONAL VALUES

GARLIC MUSHROOMS

SERVES **4**

A very popular starter to begin any meal, or to be eaten as just a light snack.

75 g butter
750 g mushrooms, button or cap
a few drops of lemon juice
salt substitute (see page 14) and freshly ground black pepper
3 tsp garlic, crushed
1 tbsp coriander or parsley, chopped

1. Heat the butter in a large pan.
2. Add the mushrooms and sweat gently, covered, for 5 minutes, shaking occasionally.
3. Add the lemon juice, salt substitute and pepper.
4. Increase the heat, tossing the mushrooms well.
5. Add the garlic, toss, and cook for 2 minutes.
6. Add the coriander or parsley and cook for 1 minute. Remove from the heat and serve.

NUTRITIONAL VALUES

CEVICHE

SERVES **4**

In this Mexican speciality the lime juice 'cooks' the fish.

450 g firm white fish fillets, skinned and cubed
100 ml lime juice
1 small onion, finely chopped
1 large tomato, peeled, deseeded and chopped
1–2 fresh green chillies, deseeded and thinly sliced
3 tbsp olive oil
1 small ripe avocado, peeled, pitted and sliced (optional)

1. Put the fish into a pretty glass bowl, pour over the lime juice, cover and leave to marinate for 4–6 hours or overnight.
2. Half an hour or so before serving, stir in the remaining ingredients, except for the avocado, and season to taste.
3. Chill briefly, and serve decorated with avocado slices, if you like.

NUTRITIONAL VALUES

MONKFISH WITH ANCHOVY SAUCE

SERVES **4**

A succulent and tasty seafood dish served in small portions as a starter.

450 g monkfish tail, skinned, cleaned and cubed

120 ml olive oil

60 ml anchovy essence

1 tbsp freshly ground black pepper

1. Season the fish.
2. Heat the oil in a pan, add monkfish pieces and lower heat.
3. Cover and cook for 4–6 minutes, until the flesh is still quite springy and very slightly underdone.
4. Remove from the sauce and keep warm.
5. Add the rest of the ingredients to the pan and bring to the boil.
6. Taste for a strong sharp peppery flavour.
7. Return the fish to the sauce, stir and serve.

NUTRITIONAL VALUES

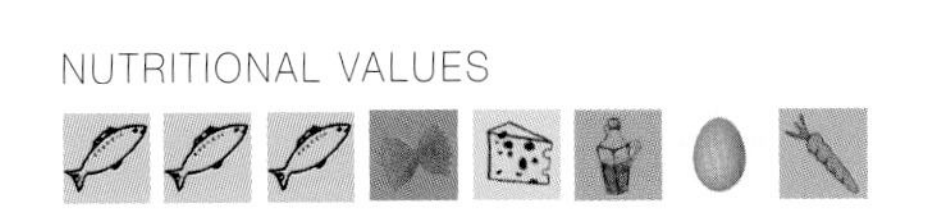

SMOKED WHITE FISH SALAD

SERVES **6**

The vodka in this recipe gives it its Russian accent – never omit it. Smoked Fish Salad is a perfect way to start a weekend brunch; it is also good as a starter for any lunch or dinner.

3 large smoked fish (trout, mackerel, haddock), cleaned and sliced open
360 ml low-fat sour cream
1 large red onion, chopped
1 tbsp fresh dill, chopped, or 1 tsp dried dill
1 tbsp vodka
freshly ground black pepper to taste
60 g watercress, chopped

1 With a fork, break the fish into large meaty chunks. Arrange the pieces on serving plates.

2 Mix the low-fat sour cream, onion and dill together in a serving bowl.

3 Garnish the dressing with a little more dill and add the vodka. Garnish the fish with watercress and serve.

NUTRITIONAL VALUES

CEVICHE OF PRAWN

SERVES **4**

A very colourful starter, served with lime to give it a kick!

- 1 kg prawns or 1/2 kg prawns and 1/2 kg white fish, skinned and cleaned
- 1.1 litres water
- 1/2 litre lime juice
- 2 red onions, chopped
- 2 tbsp soy sauce
- freshly ground black pepper
- 2 cucumbers, deseeded, skinned, halved lengthways and cut into half moons
- 1 red pepper, deseeded and thinly sliced
- 1 bunch of dill, chopped
- tabasco sauce to taste
- lime wedges to garnish

1. Place the prawns in a large bowl.
2. Mix the ingredients for the marinade together (water, lime juice, red onions, soy sauce and pepper) and pour over the prawn.
3. Marinate for 20 minutes.
4. Add the cucumber, pepper slices and dill. Toss.
5. Spoon onto plates or into small bowls.
6. Sprinkle with pepper and tabasco sauce. Serve with lime wedges.

NUTRITIONAL VALUES

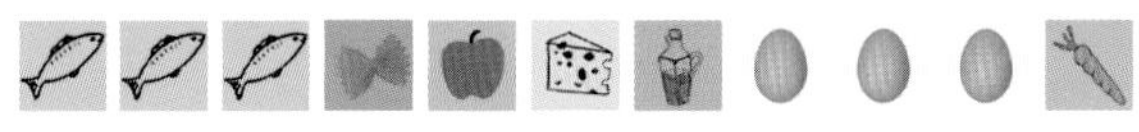

KING PRAWNS IN GARLIC

SERVES **4**

This starter is very simple to make, and the result is delicious. Alternatively, you could use larger amounts and turn this into a main course served with salad.

3 tbsp olive oil

12 king prawns, fresh if available; if not, cook from frozen

2 tsp garlic, crushed

2 tsp paprika

2 tbsp medium sherry

lemon wedges

NUTRITIONAL VALUES

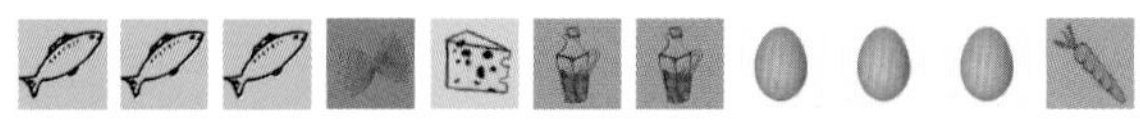

1. Heat the oil in a pot. For frozen prawns, lower heat, add the prawns to the oil, cover and cook for 6 minutes, until soft and heated through. For fresh, add to the oil until sizzling.
2. Add the rest of the ingredients and bring to the boil. Taste for seasoning.
3. Serve with lemon wedges.

SCALLOPS WITH LIME AND CRAB

SERVES **4**

This can be prepared the day before if you do not have time, then it can be left till the last minute as it is served well chilled.

12 small–medium, or 6 large scallops (slice the latter across horizontally)
juice of 4 limes
juice of 2 oranges
$1\frac{1}{2}$ tbsp brandy
1 small piece gingerroot, finely chopped
freshly ground black pepper
150 g white crab meat

NUTRITIONAL VALUES

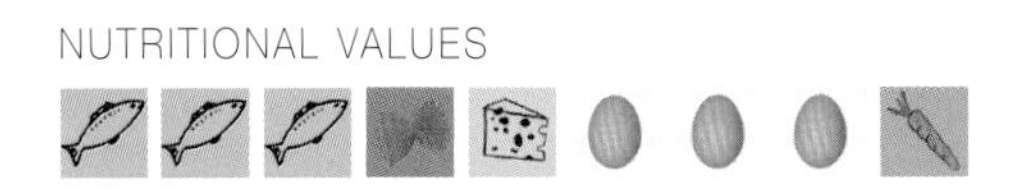

1. To pry open the scallops place them dark side of shell down and slip a sharp knife through the hinge to sever the muscle which holds the scallop to the shell.
2. Trim away the muscular 'foot'. Wash and place in the refrigerator, in the cleaned shells, on a tray.
3. Mix the lime juice, orange juice, brandy, ginger and seasoning together and spoon over the scallops. Marinate for 4–6 hours. The scallops will go opaque and be firm to the touch when ready.
4. Lightly season the crab meat and flake over the scallops.
5. Serve well chilled.

ANDALUSIAN MUSSEL SALAD

SERVES **4**

Tinned mussels may be used in this recipe, but fresh mussels are infinitely preferable. Serve this salad as a starter or a main course for lunch.

1 hard-boiled egg yolk
60 ml pure olive oil
1 clove garlic, finely chopped
60 ml white wine vinegar
1 tbsp fresh parsley, chopped
½ tsp freshly ground black pepper
125 g sweet green pepper, chopped
125 g sweet red pepper, chopped
12 oz fresh mussels, cooked and well drained
6 coarsely chopped pimento-stuffed green olives
1 medium-size onion, sliced in rings
6 black olives

1 In a small bowl, mash the egg yolk with 2 tablespoons of the olive oil and the garlic. Add the remaining olive oil and the vinegar. Stir well. Add the parsley, and pepper. Stir until well blended.

2 In a serving bowl, put the green and red peppers, mussels, and chopped green olives. Toss gently. Pour the egg dressing over the salad and toss gently again. Cover the bowl and refrigerate for 30 minutes.

3 Remove the salad from the refrigerator, garnish with the onion rings and black olives and serve.

NUTRITIONAL VALUES

AVOCADO AND PRAWN SALAD

SERVES **6**

This recipe is easily halved to serve two or three. If you do this, leave the stone of the avocado in the unused half; this will keep the avocado from discolouring.

60 ml pure olive oil
60 ml white wine vinegar
3 tbsp spring onion, chopped
1/4 tsp dried oregano
1/4 tsp Tabasco sauce
450 g cooked prawns
2 large tomatoes, deseeded and diced
1 cucumber, peeled and diced
3 tbsp pimento-stuffed green olives, coarsely chopped
3 tbsp pimento, chopped
1/2 tsp freshly ground black pepper
3 medium-size avocados
1 tbsp fresh lemon juice
6 lettuce leaves
3 tbsp fresh parsley, chopped

1 Put the olive oil, vinegar, spring onion, oregano and Tabasco sauce in a jar with tightly fitting lid. Cover tightly and shake until well mixed.

2 Put the prawns in a mixing bowl. Pour the dressing over the prawn. Toss lightly and cover. Let marinate for 1–2 hours at room temperature.

3 Add the tomato, cucumber, olives, pimento and pepper to the prawns. Toss lightly.

4 Halve the avocados and remove the stones. Sprinkle the lemon juice on the avocados to retard discolouration.

5 Line a serving platter with lettuce leaves and place the avocado halves on top. Spoon the prawn salad into and on to the avocado halves. Sprinkle with parsley and serve.

NUTRITIONAL VALUES

SALMON WITH NEW MEXICO PEPPER AND LIME

SERVES **4**

A nice creamy salmon starter which looks and tastes wonderful served with a bunch of mustard and cress.

1 tbsp olive oil
1 fresh red or green New Mexico pepper, deseeded and diced
juice of 6 limes
500 ml fish stock (see page 24)
4 x 175 g pieces salmon fillet
4 tbsp low-fat double cream

NUTRITIONAL VALUES

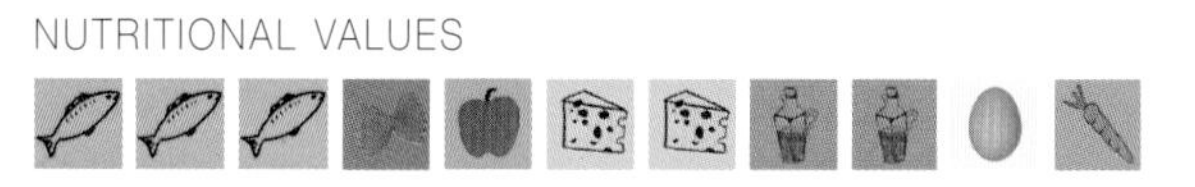

1. Heat the oil in a large frying pan. Add the pepper and sauté just until softened, 2–3 minutes. Add the lime juice and bring to the boil. Reduce until only 1–2 tablespoons of liquid remain.

2. Add the fish stock and bring to the boil. Reduce to a low simmer. Place the salmon pieces in the pan, flesh side up, and poach until firm but not overcooked, about 10 minutes. Remove salmon to a plate and refrigerate.

3. Slowly stir the low-fat cream into the poaching liquid and continue to simmer over very low heat. When the sauce begins to thicken, spoon 2 tablespoons over the cooling salmon in the refrigerator. Repeat this every few minutes until all of the sauce has been added to the fish. The sauce may be somewhat thin when you begin, but will be quite thick by the last few spoonfuls. Serve chilled.

ASPARAGUS WITH PARMESAN AND FRIED EGGS

SERVES **4**

This is a different way to serve up asparagus, you can dip the asparagus in the egg yolk so make sure you don't overcook the egg!

1 kg fresh asparagus

85 g butter

125 g Parmesan cheese, freshly-grated

2 tbsp olive oil

4 eggs

NUTRITIONAL VALUES

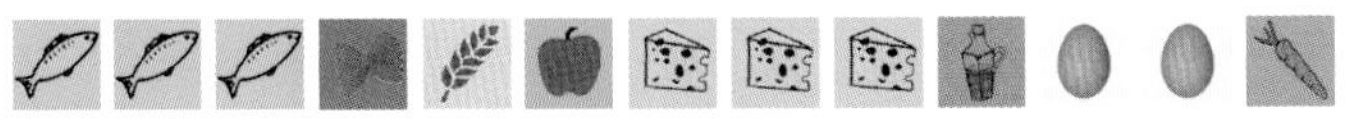

1 Preheat the oven to 190°C/gas mark 5. Trim the coarse whitish ends from the asparagus spears.

2 Boil the asparagus in water for about 10 minutes. (If you can keep the heads above the surface of the water, so much the better. Steamed, they have a better chance of remaining intact.)

3 Grease the bottom of a flat, oven-proof dish with one-third of the butter. It should be large enough to accommodate the asparagus in two layers only.

4 When the asparagus has cooked, arrange it in the dish.

5 Sprinkle the Parmesan over the asparagus and dot it with the remaining butter then bake until the cheese and butter form a light brown crust – about 10 minutes.

6 In the meantime, fry the eggs carefully. You must not break the yolks.

7 To serve, divide the asparagus into four portions on heated plates. Slide a fried egg over each portion. The crusty, cheesy asparagus is dipped in the egg yolks and eaten by hand with precious little finesse but much enjoyment.

ZESTY ASPARAGUS SALAD

SERVES **4**

The slight sharpness of the mustard in this salad accents the delicate flavour of the asparagus. To save time, the vinaigrette may be made up to two days in advance.

500 g asparagus, trimmed
4–8 large lettuce leaves
1 hard-boiled egg, finely chopped

ZESTY VINAIGRETTE

190 ml mild olive oil
2 tbsp red wine vinegar
2 tsp Dijon mustard
1/4 tsp freshly ground black pepper
1 large clove garlic, crushed
2 tbsp snipped chives

1 Soak the asparagus stalks in cold water to remove any dirt, then drain. Bring a large, shallow saucepan of water to the boil, add the asparagus, and cook for 5–7 minutes until tender-crisp. Remove each stalk with tongs; drain and rinse immediately under cold running water. Drain again, wrap in paper towels, and chill in the refrigerator for about 2 hours.

2 Prepare the vinaigrette. Place the oil, vinegar, mustard, pepper, garlic and chives in a jar with a secure lid. Shake until thoroughly blended. Refrigerate for 2 hours before using.

3 To serve, line each of four plates with 1–2 lettuce leaves. Divide the chilled asparagus between plates and spoon 1 tablespoon of vinaigrette on each plate. Sprinkle the salads with finely chopped hard-boiled egg and serve immediately.

NUTRITIONAL VALUES

SEAWEED-WRAPPED AVOCADO

SERVES **4**

Avocado is not a traditional ingredient of Japanese cooking but it is certainly popular in many Japanese homes. You can mix in wasabi, the green Japanese mustard powder, to spice up the soy sauce, which can be used as a dressing.

1 avocado
2 sheets of dried seaweed (nori)
2 tsp soy sauce
1 tsp wasabi (optional)

1 Slice the avocado in two, remove the stone and peel. Cut in half again, then slice into 1 cm widths.

2 Cut the dried seaweed into strips and wrap the avocado slices in the seaweed.

3 Pour soy sauce into a small dish. If you are using wasabi, mash in a small amount. Dip the avocado into the sauce before eating.

NUTRITIONAL VALUES

BACON-WRAPPED PRAWNS WITH LOW-FAT SOURED CREAM

SERVES **4**

This is a lovely tapa, and a very popular barbecue snack.

12 king prawns, shelled, leaving on the head and tail tip (defrost overnight if using frozen)
100 g grated Mozzarella cheese
1 tsp freshly ground black pepper
12 slices good bacon, trimmed of the rind and excess fat
a little olive oil

FOR THE DIP (SAUCE)

200 g low-fat soured cream
$^1/_2$ tsp freshly ground black pepper
juice of $^1/_2$ lemon

1. Make a slit lengthways along the back of the prawns, but do not cut through.
2. Fill the slit with the cheese, mixed with the black pepper.
3. Wrap each prawn in one strip of bacon, starting at the head, which should peep out, and slightly spiral the bacon to the tail.
4. Paint with olive oil, and either grill or bake in a hot oven, 230°C/gas mark 8, for 7–10 minutes. Meanwhile, prepare the dip.
5. Mix all the ingredients together for the sauce, and serve with the hot prawns.

NUTRITIONAL VALUES

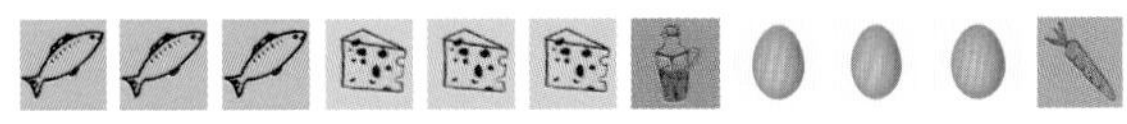

MINTED CHICKEN AND MELON MEDLEY

SERVES **4–6**

Nowadays, we are fortunate to have a variety of melons available throughout the year. This fruit contrasts well with chicken, both in flavour and moistness.

6 chicken breasts, boneless and skinned, each approximately 150 g
900 ml white grape juice
freshly ground black pepper
1/2 ripe rock melon (Charentais or Honeydew), deseeded
1/2 ripe Ogen melon, deseeded
175 g seedless red grapes
100–125 g feta cheese, cubed

DRESSING

2 tbsp light olive oil
1 tbsp grape juice
1 tbsp lemon juice
1 tbsp fromage frais or single cream
1 tbsp each freshly chopped mint and chives
freshly ground black pepper

GARNISH

fresh mint sprigs

1. Put the chicken, grape juice, and pepper to taste in a pan. Bring to the boil, then simmer for 10 minutes, or until the chicken is tender. (Turn the chicken once during cooking.) Drain and cool.
2. Using a Parisienne cutter, scoop out the flesh of the melons to form neat balls. Alternatively, cut the flesh into 2.5 cm cubes. Place in a bowl with the halved grapes. Dice the chicken and add to the fruit, together with the cheese.
3. Shake the dressing ingredients together in a screw top jar and gently fold into the salad. Chill for 30 minutes before serving, garnished with sprigs of mint.

NUTRITIONAL VALUES

CHICKEN WINGS WITH LIME JUICE AND GARLIC

SERVES **8–12**

Whenever you buy a whole chicken, freeze the wings if they are not needed. When you have enough collected in the freezer you can transform them into this deliciously tangy recipe.

12 chicken wings
4 cloves garlic, crushed
freshly ground black pepper, to taste
freshly squeezed juice of 4 limes
pinch of cayenne pepper

1. Place the chicken wings in a shallow dish. Rub the crushed garlic oil all over the chicken wings, then season with freshly ground black pepper.
2. Sprinkle the lime juice and cayenne pepper over the chicken wings, cover, and marinate in the refrigerator for 3–4 hours, turning and rearranging them occasionally.
3. Arrange the chicken wings in a large frying pan and pour the marinade over them. Add just enough cold water to cover the wings and bring quickly to the boil. Cook, uncovered, for 20–25 minutes, or until the chicken is cooked through and the sauce has reduced slightly. Serve warm or, better still, cold the next day.

NUTRITIONAL VALUES

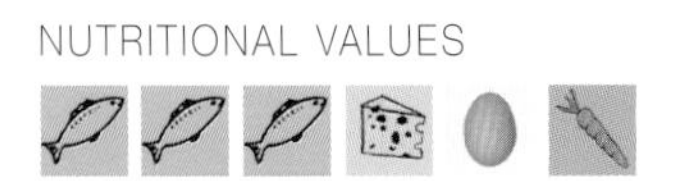

SPINACH AND CHICKEN TERRINE

SERVES **8–10**

A perfect start to a dinner party, or as a main course for a summer lunch. Serve on its own, or with a fresh crisp green salad.

SPINACH MIXTURE

500 g cooked spinach, well-drained and chopped
freshly grated nutmeg
freshly ground black pepper
150 ml low-fat fromage frais
2 egg yolks
2 tsp powdered gelatine

CHICKEN MIXTURE

1 tbsp vegetable oil
700 g boneless chicken, minced
1 clove garlic, crushed
1 tsp green peppercorns
freshly ground black pepper
4 tbsp dry Vermouth
25 g pistachio nuts
175 g fromage frais
3 tsp powdered gelatine

SAUCE

200 ml thick natural low-fat yoghurt
1 bunch watercress, washed and trimmed
1 whole clove garlic, peeled
4 tbsp dry white wine
freshly ground black pepper

GARNISH

a few green peppercorns or a sprig of dill

1. For the spinach mixture, mix the spinach with nutmeg and pepper to taste. Blend in the low-fat fromage frais and egg yolks.
2. Dissolve the gelatine in 2 tablespoons water (place in a basin over a pan of simmering water). Allow to cool slightly before stirring into the spinach mixture.
3. For the chicken mixture, heat the oil and stir-fry the minced chicken for 4–5 minutes. Do not allow it to brown.
4. Add the garlic, green peppercorns, pepper to taste and the Vermouth. Bubble briskly for 1 minute.
5. Blend the chicken in a liquidizer or food processor until smooth. Stir the pistachio nuts and low-fat fromage frais into the chicken mixture.
6. Dissolve the gelatine in 3 tablespoons water (as above) and add to the chicken mixture; blend well.
7. Put half the chicken mixture into a lightly oiled and lined 1 kg loaf pan, cover carefully with the spinach mixture, and spread the remaining chicken mixture over the top. Chill until the terrine is firm enough to slice.
8. Meanwhile, make the sauce. Put the low-fat yoghurt, watercress, and garlic into a liquidizer or food processor and blend until smooth. Stir in the white wine and season to taste.
9. Carefully unmould the set terrine and cut into slices. Place a slice on each serving plate, and spoon a pool of sauce around the terrine. Garnish with a few extra green peppercorns or a sprig of fresh dill.

NUTRITIONAL VALUES

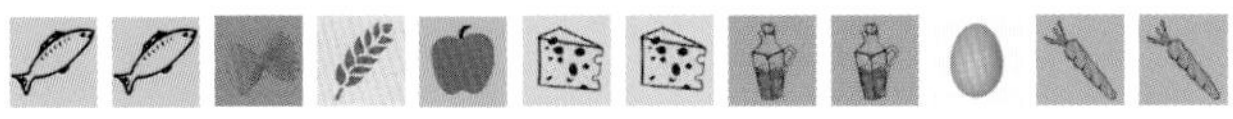

CHICKEN IN GARLIC SAUCE

SERVES **4**

This garlic sauce is the perfect accompaniment to chicken.

- 1 kg chicken wings, or 3 breasts
- 60 ml olive oil
- 25 g butter
- 1/2 glass white wine
- 3 tsp garlic, crushed
- 1 tbsp parsley, chopped
- 250 ml chicken stock (see page 24)
- 20 ml of sherry
- 20 ml of brandy
- freshly ground black pepper

1. Cut the chicken into small chunks.
2. Put the oil and butter in a pan and get them hot.
3. Put the chicken pieces in the pan, stirring quickly to seal all sides.
4. Add the wine, garlic and parsley.
5. Reduce the wine by half and add the chicken stock. Stir.
6. At this stage, the smaller pieces of chicken may be cooked; if so, remove them and put them aside.
7. Add the sherry and brandy.
8. Season and serve.

NUTRITIONAL VALUES

EGG AND OKRA SCRAMBLE

SERVES **2**

This is a tasty egg starter and is delicious when garnished with roughly chopped coriander leaves.

100 g okra
1 tbsp oil
50 g onion, chopped
1/4 tsp cumin seeds
50 g tomato, chopped
pinch of turmeric
1/4 tsp chilli powder
freshly ground black pepper
2 tsp lemon juice
3 medium-size eggs
3 cloves garlic, chopped
1 spring onion, finely chopped

1. Wash and dry the okra well. Top and tail each one then cut it into 3–4 slices.
2. Heat the oil in a medium-size non-stick frying pan with a lid. Soften the onion, then add the cumin seeds.
3. Add the okra, tomato, turmeric and chilli powder. Stir, then let the vegetables cook in their own moisture by covering the pan with its lid, over a low heat for 10–12 minutes (the okra should then be tender). Mill some black pepper over and add the lemon juice.
4. Break the eggs into a bowl and whisk with 2 tablespoons of water. Stir in the garlic and spring onion.
5. Pour the egg mixture over the vegetable mixture in the pan and, as soon as the eggs are lightly set, break up the mixture and continue to stir while it cooks. Serve immediately.

NUTRITIONAL VALUES

ASPARAGUS WRAPPED IN SMOKED SALMON

SERVES **6**

This elegant tapa is as simple to prepare as it is to eat. Always popular with guests, salmon-wrapped asparagus spears are delicious yet light, making them the ideal starter to a large main course.

6 cloves garlic, finely chopped
3 medium egg yolks
1 tspwhite wine vinegar
450 ml olive oil
lemon juice, to taste
24 asparagus spears
6 slices smoked salmon

1. First, make the alioli. Using a mortar and pestle, pound the garlic until it forms a smooth paste. One by one, thoroughly beat in the egg yolks. Mix in the vinegar. Slowly add the olive oil, drop by drop at first, increasing to a thin stream and stirring constantly once the mixture begins to thicken and emulsify. Add lemon juice to taste. Refrigerate while preparing the rest of the dish.

2. Wash and trim the asparagus spears. Bring 225 ml water to the boil and steam the asparagus, covered, for 4 minutes or until tender. Refresh the asparagus in iced water and blot dry with paper towels.

3. Cut each slice of salmon in half lengthways, to yield 12 slices. Then cut each of the 12 slices in half crossways, to yield 24 slices of salmon. Wrap each piece of salmon around each asparagus spear, making sure to leave the tip exposed. If serving as finger food, the salmon can be secured in place with a toothpick.

4. Arrange the asparagus attractively on a serving platter. The alioli may either be spooned over the asparagus, or served on the side as a dip.

NUTRITIONAL VALUES

MAIN COURSES

SWORDFISH AND HERBS WITH SMOKED BACON AND RED WINE BUTTER SAUCE

SERVES **6–8**

The combination of the fish and bacon really works well with the sauce.

1.4 kg swordfish

225 g unsmoked bacon, rind removed, cut into matchstick strips

6 tbsp fresh basil, chopped

3 tbsp fresh thyme, chopped

3 tbsp fresh chervil, chopped

3 tbsp fresh tarragon, chopped

3 tbsp olive oil

5 cloves garlic, crushed

1 tbsp freshly ground black pepper

FOR THE SAUCE

2 shallots, chopped

1 tbsp olive oil

125 ml red wine vinegar

1 tsp cracked black pepper

1 bay leaf

225 ml red wine

225 ml low-fat double cream

225 g unsalted butter, cut into small pieces and kept cold

1 Have your fishmonger cut an even-sized section of fresh boneless, skinless swordfish. Divide in half.

2 Sauté the bacon in a large frying pan until medium-rare. Remove and drain on kitchen paper. Sauté the herbs over high heat for about 1 minute to wilt. Remove from the heat and drain.

3 Using a larding needle or sharp knife, insert the bacon evenly over both sections of the swordfish. Rub the olive oil all over the fish then rub the garlic over the top of the flesh. Season with the pepper and top with the wilted herbs. Place in your cooker and smoke with the wood of your choice, for 1–1½ hours or until the fish flakes easily.

4 In a medium saucepan, stew the shallots in 1 tablespoon of olive oil. Add the vinegar, cracked black pepper and bay leaf and reduce to about 3 tablespoons. Add the red wine and reduce to 3 tablespoons. Add the low-fat double cream and reduce until it thickens. Beat in the butter, bit by bit, until it is all incorporated and strain through muslin or sieve. Keep warm.

5 Cut the swordfish into serving pieces. Place some sauce on the serving plates, top with the fish and serve. Garnish with lemon or lime wedges if liked.

NUTRITIONAL VALUES

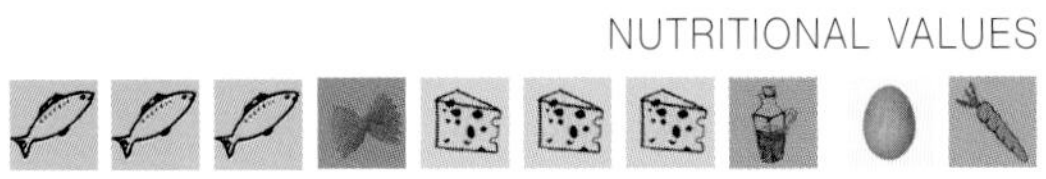

TANDOORI SOLE

SERVES **4**

A lovely spicy fish dish that can be prepared well in advance of cooking.

2 tsp cumin
$^1/_2$ tsp turmeric
$^1/_2$ tsp cloves
$^1/_2$ tsp cardamom seeds
$^1/_2$ tsp chilli powder
$^1/_2$ tsp freshly ground black pepper
$^1/_2$ tsp yellow mustard seeds
1 medium onion, chopped
2 cloves garlic, finely chopped
225ml low-fat yoghurt
6 fillets sole, skinned, or any other white fish

NUTRITIONAL VALUES

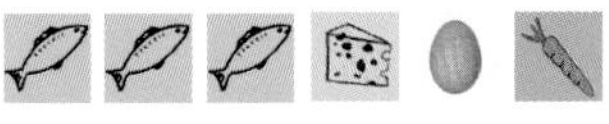

1. Grind the spices together and blend with the onion and garlic.
2. Mix into the low-fat yoghurt.
3. Marinate the fish in the low-fat yoghurt mixture for 6 hours.
4. Remove the fish from the marinade, wrap in foil, and bake for 30 minutes.

MOROCCAN FISH AND PEPPER BROCHETTES

SERVES **4**

This delicious North African dish is high in both protein, but low in carbohydrate, saturated fat and cholesterol. It also contains good levels of antioxidants.

5 cloves garlic, chopped
1/2 tsp each: paprika and cumin
several pinches cayenne pepper
6 tbsp extra-virgin olive oil
2 tbsp each fresh parsley and coriander, chopped
juice of 1 lemon
500 g firm-fleshed white fish, cut into bite-size pieces
1 each red, yellow, green pepper, peeled and cut into bite-sized pieces
1 lemon, cut into wedges

1 Combine the garlic, paprika, cumin, cayenne pepper, olive oil, 1 tablespoon of each of the parsley and coriander, and the lemon juice. Add the fish pieces and mix carefully, until thoroughly coated. Allow to marinate for 2 hours at room temperature or overnight in the refrigerator.

2 Thread onto skewers alternating with chunks of pepper.

3 Light the barbecue. Grill the brochettes over charcoal until slightly browned on each side, 7–8 minutes in total.

4 Serve sprinkled with the remaining parsley, coriander and lemon wedges. Have hot sauce on the side, for those who enjoy a spicier flavour.

NUTRITIONAL VALUES

TROUT WITH PEPPERS

SERVES **4**

Peppers are so easy to skin. Cut in half, then place skin-side up under a preheated grill and cook until the skins are charred. Remove and place in a paper bag for 10 minutes, then skin.

1 tsp unsalted butter
8 small trout fillets
freshly ground black pepper
1/4–1/2 tsp dried crushed chillies
1 red pepper, skinned and sliced
1 yellow pepper, skinned and sliced
1 shallot, peeled and sliced
1 small orange, sliced
150 ml white wine and water mixed together
1 tbsp toasted flaked almonds
fresh snipped chives, to garnish, optional
lemon-flavoured mayonnaise or Hollandaise sauce and freshly cooked vegetables or salad, to serve

NUTRITIONAL VALUES

1. Preheat the slow cooker on high and smear the inside of the cooking pot with the butter. Skin the fillets, then check that all the bones have been removed, especially the very fine pin bones. Rinse lightly and pat dry with kitchen paper.
2. Place the fillets skinned side down and season lightly with black pepper, then sprinkle with a little crushed chilli. Place 2–3 strips of each pepper on top of each fillet, then roll up and secure with cocktail sticks.
3. Place the shallot and orange in the base of the cooking pot and place the stuffed fillets on top. Pour over the wine and water. Cover, reduce the temperature to low, and cook for 2–3 hours. Remove the cocktail sticks, scatter with the almonds and garnish with the snipped chives, if using. Serve with lemon-flavoured mayonnaise or Hollandaise sauce and freshly cooked vegetables or salad.

RED MULLET PROVENCAL

SERVES **2**

Red mullet or rouget, *as it is known in France, has a very delicate taste and is best prepared simply – either by grilling or baking in foil. It has no gall and does not need to be cleaned, indeed the liver is considered a delicacy.*

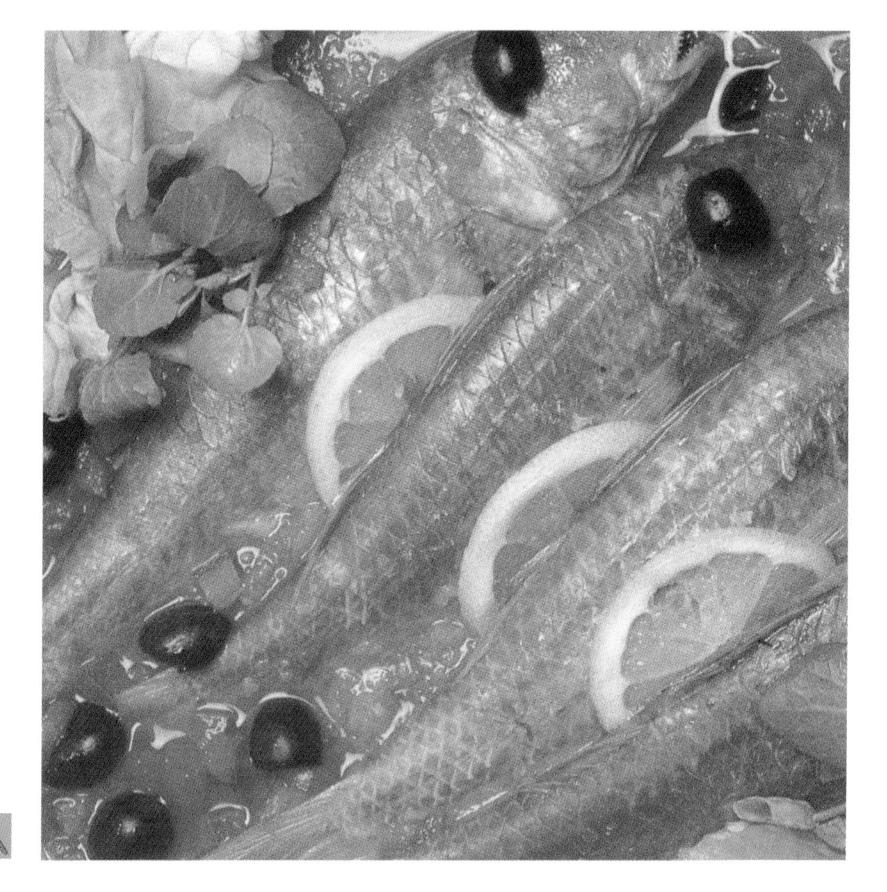

4 red mullet
2 tbsp olive oil
300 ml tomato sauce
1 green or red pepper, deseeded and diced
1 tbsp port or sherry
freshly ground pepper
stoned black olives

TO GARNISH
lemon wedges
4 anchovy fillets

NUTRITIONAL VALUES

1. Sprinkle the fish with olive oil and place under a hot grill for 2 minutes each side.
2. Arrange in an ovenproof dish.
3. Mix the tomato sauce with the diced pepper and the port. Season the fish well and pour over the sauce, then arrange the olives.
4. Bake for 20 minutes. Serve hot, garnished with lemon wedges and anchovy fillets, or serve chilled as an hors d'oeuvre.

SALMON WITH LEMON BUTTER SAUCE

SERVES **4**

This can be arranged beautifully on a plate, as a piece of edible art!

16 slim asparagus spears, trimmed
freshly ground white pepper
4 salmon fillets
1 tbsp finely chopped shallots
175 ml dry white wine
175 ml fish stock (see page 24)
2 tbsp lemon juice
250 g butter, diced

FOR THE GARNISH
salmon eggs
strips of lemon peel

1. Steam the asparagus for 12–15 minutes until tender. Blanch the strips of lemon peel for the garnish, refresh and drain and dry well.

2. Meanwhile, season the salmon and poach with the shallots in the wine and stock in a large, buttered frying pan for 8–10 minutes, until the flesh flakes easily.

3. Transfer the salmon to a warmed plate, using a pancake turner. Cover and keep warm.

4. Reduce the poaching liquid with the lemon juice to 1 tablespoon. Reduce the heat to very low and gradually beat in the butter, making sure that each piece is completely incorporated before adding the next. Season with the pepper.

5. Divide the sauce between 4 warmed plates. Place the salmon on top and place the salmon eggs on the salmon. Arrange the asparagus spears attractively on the sauce and garnish with lemon peel.

6. Serve with spinach and broccoli.

NUTRITIONAL VALUES

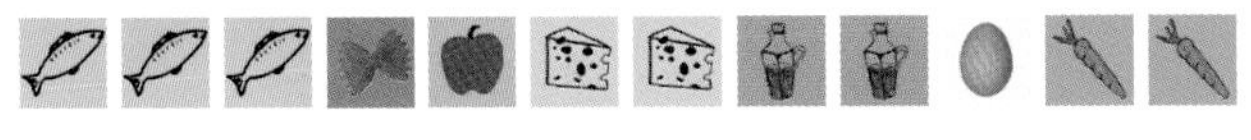

AUBERGINE AND COD BAKE

SERVES **4**

A simple bake with the flavours of the Mediterranean. This low-carb dish has good levels of soluble fibre and antioxidants.

- butter for greasing
- 2–3 tbsp olive oil
- 1 aubergine, sliced
- 1 large onion, finely sliced
- 1 clove garlic, crushed
- 1 tbsp capers
- 50 g black olives, pitted
- 500 g canned tomatoes, chopped
- 1 tbsp mixed fresh herbs, such as parsley, oregano and marjoram, chopped
- freshly ground black pepper
- 600 g cod fillet, skinned

1 Preheat the oven to 200°C/gas mark 6. Butter a 20 cm ovenproof serving dish. Heat 2–3 tablespoons of oil in a large frying pan and fry the aubergine slices gently until tender but not brown. Drain on absorbent paper towels. Add a little more oil if necessary, then add the onion and cook until softened and just starting to brown. Stir in the garlic, capers and olives, then add the tomatoes and herbs, and season to taste. Simmer the sauce for 5 minutes, until it is slightly thickened and the onions are cooked.

2 Pour the tomato sauce into the prepared dish. Divide the cod into 4 portions and add to the sauce. Cover the fish with the fried aubergine slices and dot with butter. Place the dish on a baking sheet if it seems very full and likely to bubble over, then bake in the hot oven for 20 minutes, until the aubergine slices are browned. Serve immediately.

NUTRITIONAL VALUES

FISH WITH VEGETABLES

SERVES **4**

This is cooked Bengali style. Traditionally mustard oil is used but, if you cannot find it, you can substitute any vegetable oil in its place. If you do use mustard oil, you must heat it to smoking point otherwise its pungent smell and taste will overpower the fish and can ruin the dish.

450 g haddock or cod, preferably fresh
100 g runner beans
2 tbsp oil
1/2 tsp mustard seeds
1/2 tsp cumin seeds
1/4 tsp fenugreek seeds
1 tsp grated ginger
100 g cauliflower florets
75 g tomatoes
1/2 tsp chilli powder
1/4 tsp turmeric
1/4 tsp garam masala
3–4 cloves garlic, crushed
2 tsp lemon juice
1 green chilli, chopped
2 tbsp coriander leaves

1. Wash and pat the fish dry. Cut it into 2.5 cm pieces.

2. Top and tail the beans and cut them into 1 cm lengths.

3. Heat the oil in a medium-size heavy saucepan and add the mustard, cumin and fenugreek seeds. Stir-fry them until they begin to pop and splutter.

4. Add the ginger and fry it for a minute or so. Then add the beans, cauliflower, and tomatoes, mix them in and cook for a couple of minutes.

5. Add the chilli powder, turmeric and garam masala, mix them well in, then cover the pan and cook over a low heat for 10–12 minutes.

6. Make a well in the centre of the vegetables and gently drop in the fish pieces, add the garlic, lemon juice, green chilli, and half the coriander leaves, then cover them with the vegetables. Simmer, covered, for 15–20 minutes, stirring gently halfway through.

7. Add the remaining coriander leaves, shake the pan and let it stand for a couple of minutes before serving.

NUTRITIONAL VALUES

STEAMED FISH WITH LEMON CHILLI

SERVES **4**

The combination of lemon or lime juice and fresh chillies in the topping gives this dish a refreshing spicy tartness.

500 g whole sea bass or perch, cleaned and gutted
120 ml lemon or lime juice
2 tbsp small, fresh green chillies, lightly chopped
2 tbsp garlic, chopped
2 tbsp fish sauce
10 g coriander leaves and stalks, cut into 1 cm pieces

1 Steam the fish whole for 15 minutes until tender but firm.

2 Meanwhile, mix all the remaining ingredients except the coriander, together. When the fish is cooked, place it on a serving platter and spread the lemon juice mixture all over (the fish must be very hot when the sauce is poured over).

3 Sprinkle with the coriander and serve accompanied by rice.

NUTRITIONAL VALUES

DUBLIN LAWYER

SERVES **2**

This is a traditional way to serve fresh lobster. It is essential to make it with raw lobster. Get your fishmonger to kill the lobster, cut it lengthways and remove all the meat, including the claw meat. This is difficult to do on your own at home. Make sure you keep the coral.

1 fresh lobster, about 1.2 kg, cut into chunks, together with the coral
6 tbsp butter
4 tbsp Irish whisky
150 ml low-fat cream
freshly ground black pepper

1. Heat the butter in a heavy pan until it froths, but do not brown it.
2. Cook the lobster meat and the coral lightly for a few minutes.
3. Warm the whisky, set it alight, and flame the lobster.
4. When the flames die down, add the low-fat cream. Heat for a few moments – on no account allow it to boil.
5. Place the meat and sauce back into the lobster shells. Serve on a bed of chilled lettuce.

NUTRITIONAL VALUES

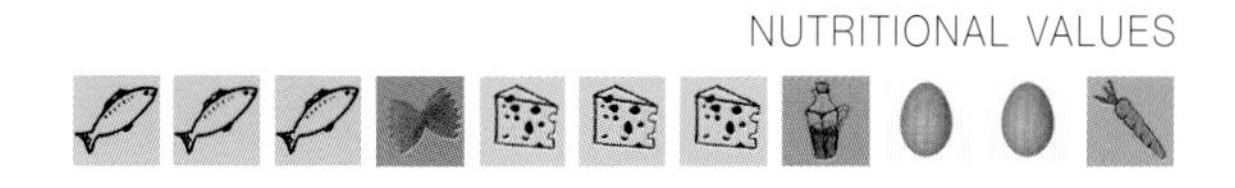

STIR-FRIED CHICKEN

SERVES **4**

Prepare the vegetables while the chicken is marinating then, once you start cooking, the recipe is soon ready to serve.

450 g skinned and boned chicken breasts, cut into strips
2 tbsp soy sauce
2 spring onions, white and some green parts, finely chopped
2.5 cm piece of fresh ginger, finely chopped
1½ tsp crushed toasted sesame seeds
freshly ground black pepper
1 small carrot, thinly sliced diagonally
3 dried Chinese black mushrooms, soaked for 30 minutes in hot water
1½ tbsp sesame oil
1 red pepper, deseeded and cut into thin strips

1. Put the chicken into a bowl.
2. Mix together the soy sauce, spring onions, ginger, sesame seeds, and plenty of pepper. Pour over the chicken, turn the chicken over and leave for 30 minutes. Remove from the marinade; reserve the marinade.
3. Meanwhile, blanch the carrot in boiling water for 5 minutes. Drain and set aside.
4. Drain the mushrooms, cut out and discard any hard patches and the stalks. Slice the mushroom caps.
5. Heat the sesame oil in a frying pan, add the chicken and stir-fry for 2–3 minutes, remove from pan and set aside. Add the mushrooms and carrots, stir-fry for 2 minutes then add the pepper and stir-fry for another minute.
6. Return the chicken to the pan, add the reserved marinade and bring to the boil. Stir and cook for 1 minute.

NUTRITIONAL VALUES

CHICKEN STUFFED WITH ARTICHOKES

SERVES **4**

This low-carb main course dish is a delicious way to serve chicken. The artichokes and the sauce are perfect accompaniments to the meat.

- 1 clove garlic
- rosemary sprig
- 2 tbsp butter
- freshly ground black pepper
- 1.5 kg chicken
- 4 cooked artichoke hearts
- 1 lemon, pierced in several places
- 4 fresh sage leaves
- 2 tbsp olive oil
- about 200 ml dry white wine

1 Preheat the oven to 180°C/gas mark 4. Crush the garlic and rosemary. Put in a bowl with the butter and pepper; mix with a wooden spoon until finely creamed.

2 Wash the chicken, pat dry and stuff with artichokes and lemon. Sew up the opening with cooking thread. Skewer the chicken together with a thin skewer, putting 1 sage leaf under each wing and each leg. Rub the butter mixture all over the chicken, then sprinkle with pepper. Put in a baking pan or dish and pour oil over. Roast for 1½ hours, turning frequently.

3 Remove from the oven when golden brown. Transfer to a serving plate and cut into pieces. Arrange the artichoke hearts around the chicken. discard the lemon. Pour the wine into the pan and heat over low heat, stirring to blend wine and dripping. Pour the sauce over the chicken and serve at once while piping hot.

NUTRITIONAL VALUES

GREEK YOGHURT CHICKEN

SERVES **6**

Chicken legs are used in this recipe, but other chicken portions work equally well. The yoghurt is used not only for flavour but also to tenderize the meat, making it more succulent and juicy.

6 chicken legs
3 cloves garlic, crushed
salt substitute (see page 14) and freshly ground black pepper, to taste
1 tsp paprika
1 tsp ground cinnamon
pinch of cayenne pepper
freshly squeezed juice of 1 lemon
8 tbsp olive oil
8 tbsp Greek yoghurt
lemon wedges, to serve

1. Place the chicken legs in a large, shallow dish. In a medium-size bowl, combine the garlic, salt substitute, freshly ground black pepper, paprika, cinnamon, cayenne pepper, lemon juice, oil and Greek yoghurt.
2. Pour the marinade over the chicken legs, stirring and turning them to coat evenly. Cover and leave to marinate in the refrigerator for 2–3 hours or overnight.
3. Season the chicken legs again with plenty of salt substitute and freshly ground black pepper. Place the chicken legs on an oiled grill rack under a preheated grill and cook for 20–40 minutes or until crisp and golden on the outside and cooked through, turning frequently during cooking. Serve with lemon wedges and a Greek salad.

NUTRITIONAL VALUES

SWEET, SOUR 'N' HOT CHICKEN

SERVES **4**

A very simple and colourful chicken dish to make, can be served on a bed of rice or as a filling for jacket potatoes.

175 g reduced sugar marmalade
100 ml lime juice
1 tsp root ginger, chopped
1 tsp ground nutmeg
dash of hot pepper or Tabasco sauce
1 tbsp vegetable oil
4 large chicken breasts (about 675 g, boned, skinned, fat cut off, cut into 2.5 cm cubes)
1 medium pawpaw (papaya), deseeded, halved, and cut into 2.5 cm cubes
175 g can sliced water chestnuts, drained
15 g fresh coriander, chopped, to garnish

1. In a small saucepan, melt the marmalade over a low heat, gradually blending in the lime juice, ginger, nutmeg and hot pepper sauce.

2. Heat the oil in a frying pan and brown the chicken cubes. Add the pawpaw (papaya) and toss for several minutes, then add the sauce and water chestnuts. Cook over a moderate heat for about 3–4 minutes until the chicken is cooked through. Taste the sauce and add hot pepper sauce to taste.

3. Spoon on to a serving dish and sprinkle with coriander.

NUTRITIONAL VALUES

MEDITERRANEAN-STYLE POUSSINS

SERVES **4**

This dish needs to be cooked on a covered barbecue, to ensure that the whole poussins are cooked through yet remain gloriously moist and succulent.

50 g unsalted butter, softened
2 slices prosciutto, finely chopped
2 tbsp rosemary, finely chopped
2 sun-dried tomatoes in oil, drained and finely chopped
2 tsp Dijon mustard
freshly ground black pepper, to taste
2 poussins, each weighing about 550–700 g
1 small lemon

1. Put the butter, prosciutto, rosemary, tomato and mustard into a small bowl and mix well.
2. Season the poussins, lightly with pepper.
3. Carefully lift the skin from the breast of each, running one or two fingers underneath to make a pocket. Spoon half the butter mixture into each pocket and smooth the skin to make a level surface.
4. Wrap each bird in oiled, heavy-duty foil, securing the seams. Grill over medium heat for about 30 minutes, turning occasionally.
5. Turn the birds breast side up and, wearing oven gloves, tear open the top of each foil parcel, completely exposing the birds but holding the juices in the foil. Cover the barbecue with the lid and continue cooking for another 15 minutes or until the poussins are golden brown and cooked through.

NUTRITIONAL VALUES

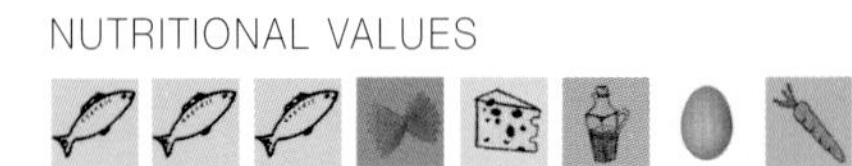

MEDITERRANEAN CHICKEN WITH FETA AND GREEN OLIVES

SERVES **4**

This dish originates from Greece. It is either prepared with olives or raisins, both of which are major products of the Mediterranean.

4 chicken breasts

freshly ground black pepper, to taste

6 tbsp olive oil

350 g button onions (or use large onions, quartered)

400 g can chopped tomatoes

400 g boiling water

275 g pitted green olives, washed and drained

1 tbsp red wine vinegar

100 g feta cheese, thinly sliced

1. Arrange the chicken breasts on a chopping board and season with freshly ground black pepper on both sides.
2. Heat the oil in a large, deep frying pan and add the chicken breasts, skin-side down. Cook on both sides for 3–5 minutes or until browned. Lift the chicken breasts out of the pan and set aside.
3. Add the onions to the frying pan and sauté for about 5 minutes or until softened, stirring frequently. Return the chicken to the pan and add the chopped tomatoes and boiling water. Season with freshly ground black pepper, cover, and simmer for 25–30 minutes or until the chicken is tender and cooked through, adding a little extra boiling water if necessary.
4. In the last 10 minutes of the cooking time, add the green olives and red wine vinegar. Stir to combine. Place a slice of feta cheese on top of each piece of chicken and continue to cook, uncovered, for a further 10 minutes, or until the cheese has just melted. Serve immediately with a Greek salad.

NUTRITIONAL VALUES

DUCK BRAISED WITH TURNIPS

SERVES **4**

This is a very tasty and warming dish.

1 duckling, weighing about 1.4 kg
4 tbsp olive oil
150 ml white wine
450 ml meat stock
100 g turnips
20 peeled button (pearl) onions
freshly ground black pepper to taste

1 Preheat the oven to 180°C/gas mark 4. Cut the duck into quarters.

2 Warm the oil over a medium heat and brown the duck quarters on each side – about 2 minutes a side in a pan you have a lid for. Pour off the fat into a second pan, increase the heat and add the white wine and stock to the duck. Cover the dish and set it to bake.

3 If you have the inclination, you can carve your turnips into olive shapes. Otherwise, cut them into chunks, unless the turnips are baby ones. Braise them over a high heat for 3–4 minutes in the oil and duck juices, then set aside. Braise the peeled onions for the same time in the same juices.

4 Add the turnips and onions to the duck and finish cooking until tender. (The duck will take about 1 hour to cook. Add the turnips and onions when you're 30 minutes in.)

5 When everything is ready, remove the duck, turnips, and onions and set aside in a warm place. Boil the juices down hard to a coating consistency. Season.

6 Arrange the duck and vegetables on a serving dish, pour over the sauce and enjoy it.

NUTRITIONAL VALUES

DUCK BREAST WITH GINGERY BALSAMIC-ORANGE SAUCE

SERVES **2–4**

Duck – whether wild or domestic – is delicious and tastes best when cooked to medium-rare. This sauce is a perfect complement for the flavourful grilled duck.

1 large duck breast, skinned
125 ml fresh orange juice
350 ml chicken stock (see page 24)
50 ml balsamic vinegar
2 tsp root ginger, shredded
50 g unsalted butter
1/2 tsp salt substitute (see page 14)
1 tsp freshly ground black pepper
1 tsp orange zest
2 tbsp olive oil
3 oranges, thickly sliced

1 Rinse the duck and pat dry with paper towels. Set aside.

2 Combine the orange juice and chicken stock in a pan over medium-high heat. Bring to the boil and, uncovered, reduce by half, which will take about 15 to 20 minutes. Add the balsamic vinegar and ginger and cook for 2–3 minutes more. While constantly whisking, add the butter, 1 tablespoon at a time. After the butter is completely incorporated, add the salt substitute, pepper and zest.

3 Brush the duck breast with the oil. Grill over hot heat. For medium-rare duck, grill 5–8 minutes per side, or until done as you desire. Grill the orange slices until they soften and char slightly.

4 Serve the duck on a bed of griddled orange slices, with the sauce poured over.

NUTRITIONAL VALUES

HOT CHINESE DUCK AND ONION SALAD

SERVES **2**

This elegant salad is almost a cross between a salad and a stir-fry.

2 duckling breast fillets
8 to 10 spring onions, trimmed
2.5 cm piece ginger root, peeled and shredded
1 clove garlic, chopped fine
2 fresh red chillies, shredded fine
1/2 Chinese cabbage, shredded
2 small heads bok choy, trimmed and shredded
1 tbsp sesame seeds
4 tbsp dark soy sauce
2 tbsp dry sherry

1 Preheat the oven to 220°C/gas mark 7. Roast the breast fillets in the hot oven for 25–30 minutes, depending on how pink you like the meat.

2 Cut deeply lengthways into both ends of 4–6 spring onions. Place in a bowl of cold water to curl. Roughly chop the remaining spring onions.

3 Prepare all the remaining vegetables.

4 Heat a wok, add the sesame seeds, and dry-fry for a few seconds until toasted. Reserve until required.

5 Allow the duck to stand for 5 minutes or so, spooning off 2 tablespoons of the fat into the hot wok. Quickly stir-fry the ginger and garlic for a few seconds until fragrant, then add the chopped spring onions and cook for a further 1 minute. Stir in the chillies, cabbage, and bok choy and stir-fry for a further 2–3 minutes. Add the sesame seeds, toss well, then scoop out with a slotted spoon and pile onto two warmed plates.

6 Add the soy sauce to the wok with the sherry and bring to the boil. Meanwhile, quickly shred the duck meat and scatter it over the vegetables. Pour the dressing over the salad, then garnish with the onion curls. Serve immediately.

NUTRITIONAL VALUES

MARINATED QUAIL

SERVES **2–4**

Served with salad and a delicious papaya-chilli vinaigrette.

8 quail, dressed

FOR THE MARINADE

250 ml olive oil

1 tsp each turmeric and mild paprika

1 clove garlic, crushed

½ tsp white pepper

assorted green salad leaves

FOR THE VINAIGRETTE

1 roasted Serrano chilli, peeled, deseeded and finely chopped

1 small pawpaw (papaya), peeled, deseeded, and diced

225 ml olive oil

3 tbsp Champagne vinegar

1. Heat the oil in a small saucepan until warm. Add the garlic and pepper and remove from the heat. Add the turmeric and paprika and leave to cool.

2. Place the quail in a non-reactive bowl or dish and pour the marinade over them, making sure all are coated. Cover and marinate for 1–3 hours in the refrigerator.

3. Remove the quail from the marinade; reserve the marinade to baste with. Place the quail on your cooker and smoke for 1–2 hours, until tender, basting with the reserved marinade.

4. To make the vinaigrette, combine the Serrano and pawpaw (papaya) in a bowl and mix well. Place half of the chilli-pawpaw (papaya) mixture in a bowl with the olive oil and vinegar and blend well. Reserve the other half of the mixture.

5. To serve, place 2 quail on a serving plate with salad topped with vinaigrette. Garnish with the rest of the chilli-paw paw (papaya) mixture.

NUTRITIONAL VALUES

SAUTÉED PHEASANT IN CREAM SAUCE

SERVES **8**

This dish looks very appetizing when served with red cabbage and fine green beans.

100 g butter
2 young pheasants, each weighing about 1 kg
450 ml low-fat double cream
4 tbsp meat glaze
450 g mushrooms
freshly ground black pepper to taste

1. Melt half the butter in a frying pan large enough to hold the pheasants.
2. Quarter each pheasant and sauté, at first over a high heat. After 3–4 minutes, cooking, turn the pieces. Cook for a further 3–4 minutes, then turn down the heat. (You should fry at a temperature hot enough to sizzle but not hot enough to burn the butter.)
3. Turn the pieces again after 10 minutes, fry for a further 10 minutes, then set aside in a warm place.
4. Add the cream and the meat glaze to the pan juices and boil hard into a thick sauce. Season if necessary.
5. As the cream is reducing, fry the mushrooms in the remaining butter.
6. Arrange the pheasant pieces on a serving dish, pour over the sauce and garnish with the mushrooms.

NUTRITIONAL VALUES

PIGEON WITH ONION, BACON AND MUSHROOMS

SERVES **4**

This most delicious and creamy sauce with bacon and mushrooms complements the pigeon well.

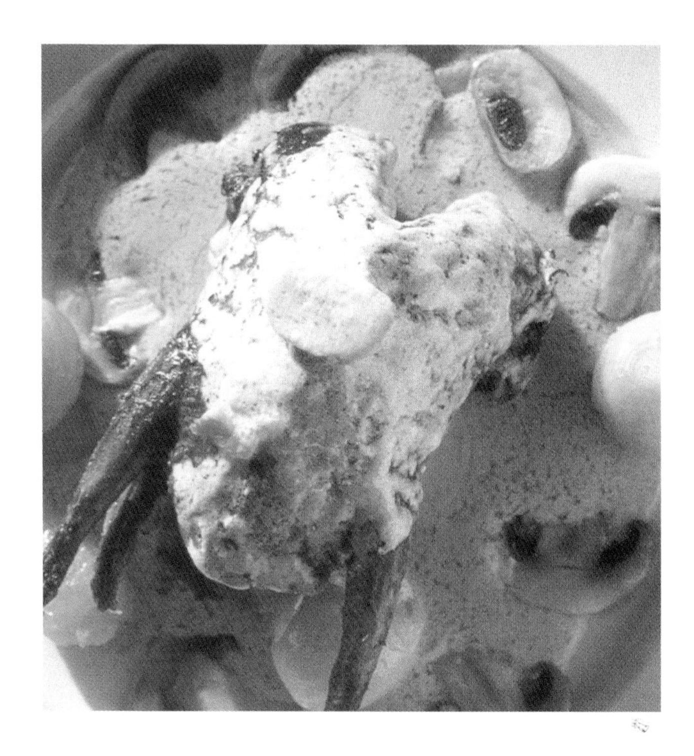

4 tbsp butter
2 plump- young pigeons
20 button (pearl) onions
2 slices lean bacon
150 ml white wine – dry or sweet
150 ml meat or game stock
225 g mushrooms
150 ml low-fat double cream
pepper to taste

NUTRITIONAL VALUES

1. Preheat the oven to 180°C/gas mark 4. Melt the butter over a high heat on top of the stove until foaming.
2. Add the whole pigeons and reduce the heat to medium. Brown on each side for 1–2 minutes. Remove them from the pan and reserve.
3. Peel the onions and cut the bacon into dice. Add them to the pan and fry both until light brown.
4. Add the wine and the stock and replace the pigeons. Cover and braise in the oven for about 30 minutes.
5. Meanwhile, wash and slice the mushrooms; after 30 minutes, add them to the cooking pigeons. (Take this opportunity to skim the cooking juices if you need to.)
6. Cook the pigeons and sauce for a further 15 minutes, then take out the pigeons. Pour the cooking juices into a frying pan on a very high heat. Add the low-fat double cream and boil the sauce hard until it's as thick as you like it – which should take no more than 10 minutes. Check the seasoning, pour over the pigeons, and serve pronto.

SAUTÈ DE VEAU

SERVES **6**

Serve this with steamed courgettes, sprinkled with chopped fresh coriander and drizzled with a little olive oil. Veal flank may be prepared in the same way.

2 large onions
3 salt-preserved lemons
2 tbsp olive oil
1 kg shoulder of veal, cubed
150 ml veal or chicken stock (see page 24)
1 tbsp coriander seeds
freshly ground black pepper
24 small black olives, pitted

NUTRITIONAL VALUES

1. Peel the onions and cut them into eight wedges. Cut the lemons into quarters and scrape away the flesh with a spoon so that only the rind remains.

2. Heat the olive oil in a cast-iron casserole dish on the stove and brown the veal cubes evenly, a few at a time. When they are all browned, return them to the casserole dish with the onions and the lemon rind juices, turn down the heat, cover, and wait until the meat, onions and lemons start to produce a liquid.

3. Pour in the stock, add the coriander seeds, and season with the black pepper. Cover again and allow to simmer gently for $^{3}/_{4}$ hour over a low heat.

4. About 10 minutes or so before the veal is cooked, add the pitted olives.

CHUNKED PORK IN ORANGE SAUCE

SERVES **4**

Pork tastes really good in an orange sauce and this can be served with a variety of vegetables.

60 g olive oil
1 small onion, finely sliced
600 g pork fillet, cut into 2.5 cm cubes
grated rind of 2 oranges
juice of 3 oranges
190 ml chicken broth (see page 24)
2 green chillies, chopped, or 2 tsp chilli paste
1 tsp garlic, crushed
1 tbsp coriander or parsley, chopped
1 tbsp cold water
freshly ground black pepper
parsley, to garnish

1 In a large frying pan, heat the oil. Sauté the onion until soft and golden, and place aside.

2 Add the pork to the pan and cook, turning until it is browned on all sides.

3 Combine the orange rind, orange juice, broth, chilli, garlic,and coriander or parsley together, and pour over the pork. Bring to the boil and add the onion slices. Simmer for 10 minutes. Place in a warm bowl.

4 Simmer to reduce and thicken. Stir, season and pour over the meat. Garnish with parsley and serve.

NUTRITIONAL VALUES

SAUTÉED LAMB WITH AUBERGINE IN A SAUCE

SERVES **4**

These cutlets look great served garnished with lemon slices and sprigs of fresh mint.

2 large aubergines, ends cut off and thickly sliced

3 tbsp olive oil

8 lamb cutlets, trimmed

2 cloves garlic, trimmed

6 large tomatoes, blanched, skinned and thickly sliced

freshly ground black pepper

1 lemon, sliced, to garnish

sprigs of mint, to garnish

NUTRITIONAL VALUES

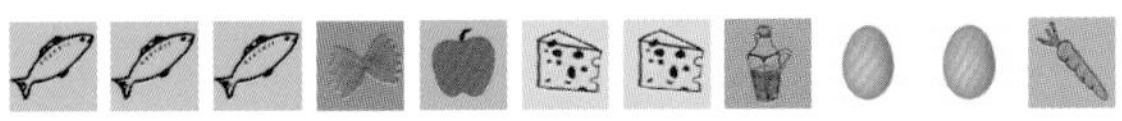

SAUCE

2 tbsp chopped fresh mint

170 ml natural unsweetened low-fat yoghurt

freshly ground black pepper

1. Rinse the sliced aubergine and dry with absorbent paper towels.

2. Heat 2 tablespoons of olive oil in a wok or large frying pan over a very high heat and add the lamb cutlets. When the meat is brown, lower the heat and continue to cook until the meat is tender, which will take about 5 minutes on each side. Remove the cutlets from the wok, drain on absorbent paper towels, and keep warm in the oven.

3. Add the remaining oil to the wok and fry the aubergine slices with the garlic until they are lightly browned on both sides. If the oil dries out, add a little more. When the aubergine is cooked, push the slices up the sides of the wok and add the tomato slices. Stir-fry for a few moments and season with pepper.

4. To make the sauce, stir the mint into the yoghurt and grind over some black pepper. Serve in a small bowl.

5. Place the vegetables on a dish and arrange the cutlets over them. Serve garnished with lemon slices and sprigs of fresh mint.

GIGOT À LA AIL AUX OLIVES

SERVES **6**

Leg of lamb, French style, with whole cloves of garlic and olives. Aioli is a nice accompaniment to this dish.

1.8 kg leg of lamb
rosemary or thyme, fresh or dried, as desired
8 cloves garlic, cut into slivers
2 heads garlic, with cloves separated but not peeled
4–6 tbsp extra virgin olive oil
freshly ground black pepper, as desired
250 ml chicken stock (see page 24)
250 ml red wine
several handfuls of flavourful olives of choice, either green or black
1–2 tbsp fresh, chopped parsley or other fresh herbs, such as marjoram

NUTRITIONAL VALUES

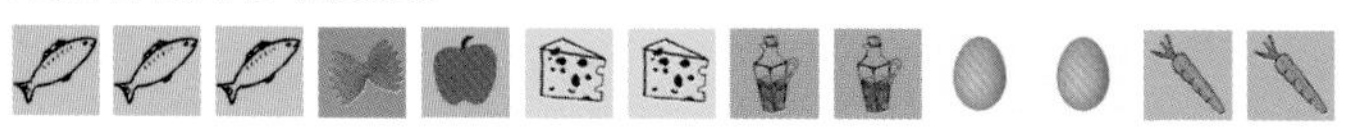

1. Make incisions all over the lamb, and into each incision place a pinch of thyme or rosemary and a sliver or two of garlic. Place the lamb in a roasting pan and surround it with the whole garlic cloves. Drizzle 4 tablespoons of olive oil over the lamb, and sprinkle with any leftover, slivered garlic and pepper.

2. Roast, uncovered, at 180°C/gas mark 4 in the oven until the lamb reaches an inner temperature of 50°C. (Note: if you have a gas oven, you'll need to measure the temperature with a special oven thermometer, which are available in many shops.) The lamb should be pink. This is an excellent time to use a meat thermometer, to check the meat's internal temperature.

3. Remove from the oven and place the meat on a platter to keep warm. Skim the fat from the pan, and add the stock and red wine. Boil down until the sauce has reduced by about half and is very flavourful, then add the olives, and warm through.

4. Serve the lamb sliced and surrounded by the roasted garlic-and-olive sauce, and a sprinkling of chopped parsley or herbs.

GRILLED BUTTERFLIED LEG OF LAMB

SERVES **8–10**

This is a wonderful recipe for lamb, combining the complementary flavours of garlic and rosemary to delicious effect.

One 2.25–3 kg leg spring lamb, deboned and butterflied (ask your butcher to do this)
8 cloves garlic, thinly sliced
4 tbsp rosemary, finely chopped
50 ml olive oil
juice of 2 lemons
2 tsp freshly ground black pepper
3 sprigs fresh rosemary

1. Combine all the ingredients except the lamb in a small bowl.

2. Rub the marinade all over the lamb. Place in a glass baking dish or resealable plastic bag and let the lamb marinate in the refrigerator for 2–4 hours, or overnight.

3. Remove the lamb from the refrigerator 30 minutes before grilling.

4. Begin grilling over hot heat to sear the lamb, 5 to 7 minutes per side. Depending upon the type of griller you are using, either turn the grill down to medium-hot, or spread out the coals so your fire cools to medium-hot. Grill the lamb for 30 to 40 minutes, covered if your grill has a lid, turning often. For medium-rare, cook until the internal temperature reaches 55 to 58°C. (Note: if you have a gas oven, you'll need to measure the temperature with a special oven thermometer, which are available in many shops.) Or, cook until done to your liking. Serve with fresh rosemary sprigs as garnish.

NUTRITIONAL VALUES

ROAST FILLET MIGNON WITH COURGETTE

SERVES **4**

Cooked in this way, the beef will still be rare but the juices will spread back evenly through the meat resulting in a smooth pink colour all over except for the outside crust. The sauce makes this a sophisticated dish.

1.5 kg centre piece of fillet mignon
cooked marinade (see recipe, right)
50 g butter
4 courgettes, cut into strips with a vegetable peeler
100 g sliced mushrooms
pepper
1 tbsp redcurrant jelly
2 tsp tomato purée
400 g beef consommé

FOR THE MARINADE

375 ml red or white wine
4 tbsp wine vinegar
1 onion, sliced
1 carrot, diced
1 celery stalk, sliced
12 black peppercorns, crushed
6 juniper berries, crushed
3 tbsp vegetable oil
4 tbsp olive oil

NUTRITIONAL VALUES

1 To make the marinade, simmer all the ingredients together except for the olive oil for 20 minutes. Cool. Strain while still just warm then whisk in the olive oil. This marinade tenderizes the meat.

2 Trim the meat of all sinews and marinate it overnight. The next day drain and pat dry on paper towels. Reserve the marinade.

3 Put the butter in a heavy pan and heat until it starts to brown. Gently fry first the courgette strips, drain them, and set aside, and then, separately, the mushrooms. Drain and set aside. Season the meat and place in the pan, turning it so it browns evenly all over, seasoning it generously with freshly ground black pepper as you do so. This should take about 10 minutes. Place the meat in an oven set to 110°C/gas mark ¼ to rest and finish cooking. (Note: if your gas oven doesn't have a setting of gas mark ¼, you'll need to measure the temperature with a special oven thermometer, which are available in many shops.)

4 Meanwhile, strain the marinade into the pan and reduce it to 1–2 tablespoons. Add the jelly and tomato purée and stir until dissolved completely into the sauce. Pour in the consommé and simmer to reduce and thicken.

5 Bring to the boil, add the mushrooms, and simmer gently for 1–2 minutes. Check the seasoning and reheat the courgette slices. Place the steak on a serving dish, pouring any residual juices into the sauce, garnish with the courgette strips, and carve into thick slices at table. Serve the sauce separately.

GRILLED ENTRECÔTE STEAKS WITH RED WINE SAUCE

SERVES **4**

This is a modern reworking of a classic French recipe, in which the red wine sauce, known as sauce Marchand de vin, *was thickened with a roux – a cooked mixture of melted butter and flour used to thicken sauce – though it still needs to be reduced for a long time.*

1 small carrot

1 small onion

1 celery stick

1 medium tomato

2 shallots

5 tbsp unsalted butter

1 sprig thyme

500 ml veal or beef stock

250 ml red wine

2 entrecôte (boned rib) steaks, each weighing 350–400 g

freshly ground black pepper

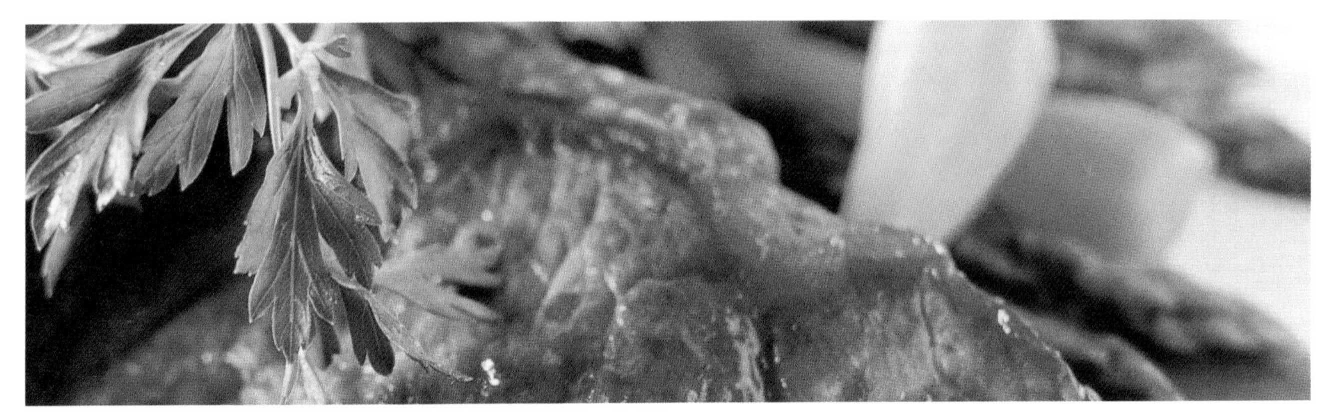

1. First, prepare the stock for the sauce: peel the carrot and the onion, trim the celery stick, and chop them all coarsely. Chop the tomato. Peel the shallots, chop them, and set aside.

2. Warm 1 tablespoon oil in a saucepan and brown the chopped vegetables except the tomato. Add the thyme, tomato, and the veal or beef stock and allow to simmer gently for 45 minutes. After this time, strain the vegetables and set aside, reserving the liquor. Boil the liquor to reduce it to a syrupy consistency.

3. Bring the red wine to the boil in a small saucepan and cook until reduced by half.

4. Grill the entrecôtes for 5 minutes each side then transfer to a plate, cover with another plate, and keep warm.

5. Warm 1 tablespoon oil in a small saucepan, add the shallots, the reduced wine, and the stock; when the mixture thickens, lower the heat and add the remaining oil, whisking it to bind the sauce.

6. Season, slice, and garnish the entrecôtes with chopped parsley. Pour the sauce over the entrecôtes, and serve with asparagus and baby carrots.

NUTRITIONAL VALUES

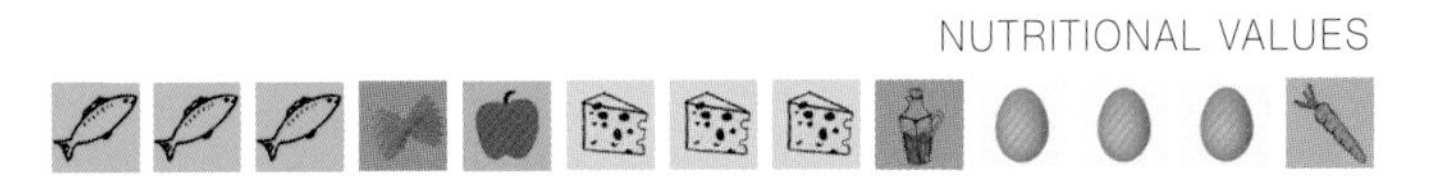

GRILLED CREOLE COMBO SKEWERS

SERVES **4**

Seafood, steak and chicken unite to make wonderful kebabs, brushed with a pungent, spicy seasoning before being barbecued to tender perfection.

8 king prawns
250 g sirloin or rump steak, cut into 2.5 cm cubes
225 g boneless, skinless chicken breast, cut into 2.5 cm cubes
225 g monkfish cut into 2.5 cm cubes
3 tbsp olive oil
1–2 tsp chilli oil
1 tbsp lemon juice
1 tsp Worcestershire sauce
4 green onions, finely chopped
1 plump garlic clove, crushed
1 small celery stick, finely chopped
finely grated rind of 1/2 a lemon

1 Peel the prawns, leaving the tails intact. Divide the prawns, steak, chicken and monkfish into four portions and thread each portion onto a flat metal skewer.

2 Mix the remaining ingredients together and brush the mixture over the kebabs. Leave to stand for 10 minutes then brush again.

3 Transfer to the barbecue and cook over medium–high heat for about 8–10 minutes, turning occasionally, or until the prawns and chicken are cooked through and the steak and fish are just tender. Serve immediately.

NUTRITIONAL VALUES

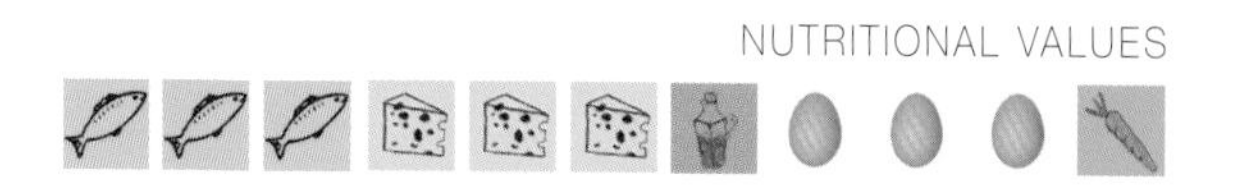

GRILLED STEAK WITH A MUSTARD CRUST

SERVES **4**

The marinade becomes crusty as it cooks, making a pungent, crisp topping. A splendid lunch dish to eat with salad.

4 rump steaks, weighing 200 g each
2 tbsp olive oil

MUSTARD MARINADE

4 tbsp olive oil
2 tsp freshly ground black pepper
2 cloves garlic, crushed
4 tbsp wholegrain Dijon mustard
2 tsp brown sugar
2 tsp ground ginger

NUTRITIONAL VALUES

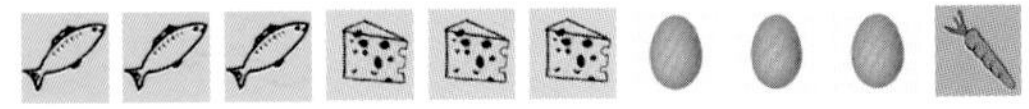

1. Mix the marinade ingredients together, adding a few drops of water if necessary, to form a thick paste.

2. Marinate the steaks in this mixture in a plastic bag for a couple of hours in the fridge. Remove the steaks from the bag and scrape any excess marinade back into it. Preheat the grill.

3. In the meantime seal the steaks in the oil for 2 minutes each in a hot pan, smear over the marinade, and place under the grill to form a crust. Transfer to warmed plates, pour over the buttery juices from the pan and serve with a green salad.

HANGING STEAK

SERVES **4**

This steak, also called boxeater or back rolls, is not often found. The meat, which is exceptionally juicy, has a dark colour and an almost striplike appearance. Do not be put off by this; the unprepossessing exterior hides a sublime flavour.

4 hanging (back roll) steaks or 2 whole muscles, weighing 275 g each
salt substitute (see page 14) and freshly ground black pepper
olive oil, to brush
lemon rind, to garnish

NUTRITIONAL VALUES

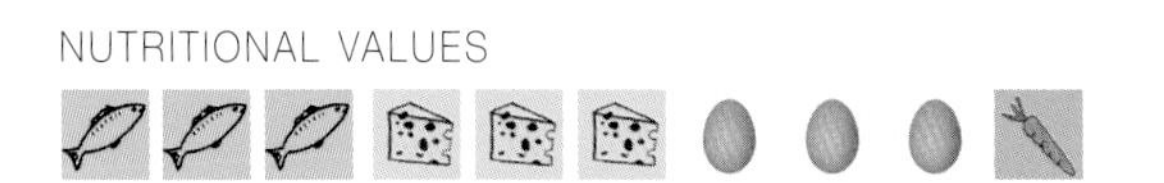

1 Preheat the grill or barbecue. If the steak has not been prepared, remove all fat and sinew and rinse it well. Pat dry with paper towels. Remove the centre sheet of gristle and divide the muscle into two individual lobes.

2 Brush the steaks with some oil and season. Place them under the grill or the barbecue, turning them frequently, so they cook evenly all round. This will take about 10 minutes. Lift out and carve into slices against the grain. Do not overcook or they will become tough. Serve with a salad or vegetable of your choice.

BACHI'S BEEF, ONION AND GREEN PEPPER PATTIES

SERVES **4**

This marvellous, simple dish of minced beef patties cooked with onions and peppers is bound to become a family favourite.

500 g lean ground beef
3–4 cloves garlic, coarsely chopped
1 onion, finely chopped
1–2 tbsp vegetable oil, if needed
3 to 4 onions, thinly sliced
3 cloves garlic, thinly sliced
3 green peppers, thinly sliced
soy sauce to taste

1. Mix the meat with the chopped garlic and the chopped onion and form it into small but thick patties.
2. Heat the oil in a frying pan, add the patties, and brown quickly on each side over medium-high heat. Add the onions, sliced garlic, peppers and soy sauce to taste, then reduce the heat and cook, covered, over a low heat for about 20 minutes, turning once halfway through the cooking time.
3. You should have browned patties, onions and peppers cooked together with a very small amount of liquid. If the onions and peppers are not browned well enough, remove the meat and sauce and allow the onions and peppers to brown before serving everything together. For extra 'bite' you could dust the dish with a sprinkling of paprika.

NUTRITIONAL VALUES

ROAST RIB OF BEEF WITH BEARNAISE SAUCE

SERVES **4**

The aroma from this dish is almost as good as the taste, and all part of the enjoyment. If you like, serve with a spoonful of plain low-fat yoghurt.

1.75 kg beef rib

freshly ground black pepper

100 g unsalted butter

FOR THE BEARNAISE SAUCE

225 g unsalted butter, cut into cubes

4 shallots or green onions, finely chopped

3 tbsp white wine vinegar

2 tbsp fresh tarragon, chopped

½ tsp chopped chervil

pinch of freshly ground black pepper

4 egg yolks

2 tbsp cold water

1. Season the rib of beef with pepper and place in a heavy roasting pan. Melt the butter and cook in a hot oven, browning the meat on both sides. For rare meat, cook for 10 minutes per pound on each side. Remove the mat to a serving platter and keep warm.

2. To make the sauce, in a small heavy saucepan melt 1 tablespoon of butter. Add the shallots. Cook slowly for about 10 minutes, then add the vinegar, half the tarragon and chervil, and pepper to taste. Reduce the sauce to about 2 tespoons.

3. Cool the mixture and add the egg yolks and the cold water. Mix with a whisk over a low heat or in a double boiler or saucepan. Make sure you amalgamate the eggs with the shallot mixture, but do not cook them or the sauce will be ruined.

4. When the egg yolks look thick and creamy, gradually whisk the remaining butter in, making sure the sauce does not separate. If it gets too thick, add a little water.

5. When the sauce is finished, add more chopped tarragon and chervil. Keep warm in the double boiler or double saucepan. (If the worst happens and the sauce separates, start again with a little water in a saucepan. Heat it continuously, adding small quantities of the sauce until it emulsifies again.)

6. Carve the ribs and serve the sauce separately.

NUTRITIONAL VALUES

STEAK WITH WILD MUSHROOMS

SERVES **4**

Avoid washing the wild mushrooms. They are such delicate fungi that they lose flavour and character if they become water-laden. It is best to brush them clean gently with a pastry brush.

5 cm thick fillet steaks, weighing 180–225 g each
150 g unsalted butter
1 shallot, chopped
250 ml red wine
250 ml beef consommé
100 g fresh wild mushrooms (preferably girolles), cleaned and trimmed
salt substitute (see page 14) and freshly ground black pepper
12 baby onions and sauce soubise, to garnish

1 Preheat the oven to 230°C/gas mark 8. Brown the fillets over very high heat in a frying pan or chargrill them for 2 minutes on both sides. Place them in a roasting tin and cook in the oven for 5 minutes. Allow to rest in a warm place until you are ready to serve.

2 Meanwhile, melt 50 g butter in a pan, add the shallots and wine, and boil fiercely until the shallots have absorbed the wine. Pour in the consommé and simmer for 5 minutes. Stir well and bring to the boil again to allow the sauce to thicken.

3 In a sauté pan gently fry the wild mushrooms in the remaining butter, season, and lift out. To remove the pieces of shallot, strain the sauce into the pan, mix well, and season as necessary.

4 Return the steaks to the pan or grill to reheat and pour any juices that have oozed out of them into the sauce. Turn them and cook for a further 30 seconds on the other side and then slice them in half across and arrange each one with the cut side uppermost on a hot plate. To serve, pour the sauce around, arrange the mushrooms attractively, and garnish with the baby onions in sauce soubise.

NUTRITIONAL VALUES

DESSERTS

CRÈME CARAMEL

SERVES **6**

This is a very light and tasty custard dessert that can also be served with fruit.

450 ml milk

1 vanilla pod

225 g sugar substitute

2 eggs

4 egg yolks

NUTRITIONAL VALUES

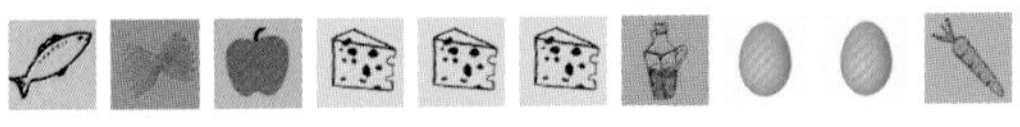

1. Heat the milk to boiling point and remove from the heat. Add the vanilla pod and allow it to steep.
2. As the vanilla is infusing, dissolve half the sugar in 285 ml water. Boil the sugar and water over a high heat, until the mixture begins to brown – that is, caramelize.
3. When the mixture is a light brown, remove the pan from the heat – it will go on colouring by itself.
4. Mix the remaining sugar with the eggs and the egg yolks and beat well. Trickle in the hot milk.
5. Distribute equal quantities of the caramel mixture between 6 ramekins large enough to hold all the milk mixture. Spread the caramel evenly about the bases if you can.
6. Pour some of the milk mixture into each of the ramekins.
7. Poach the ramekins uncovered in a water bath in the oven (170°C/gas mark 3) for 35 minutes.
8. Chill before serving – in the ramekins or turned out onto a plate.

SWEET WHISKY OMELETTE

SERVES **4**

A sweet variation on the traditional omelette.

3 eggs, separated

1 tbsp butter

1 tbsp sugar substitute

2 tbsp whisky

2 tbsp Cointreau

2 tsp sifted icing sugar

NUTRITIONAL VALUES

1 Whisk the egg yolks until creamy and, in a separate bowl, whisk the whites until stiff. Fold the yolks into the whites. Melt the butter in a frying pan and pour in the mixture. Cook gently for 5 minutes. Place under a preheated grill for 2–3 minutes or until set. Sprinkle with sugar and liquor. Heat for 1–2 minutes. Scatter icing sugar over the top of the omelettete and serve immediately.

FROZEN BLOOD ORANGE SOUFFLÉ

SERVES **4**

This soufflé boasts a lovely citrus flavour good enough to complement any main course.

4 large blood oranges

4 tbsp Grand Marnier or other orange liqueur

100 g sugar substitute

1 tbsp powdered gelatine

3 medium-size egg whites

pinch of salt substitute (see page 14)

250 ml low-fat double cream

1 Cut six 15 cm long pieces of greaseproof paper (make sure they are large enough to extend around the rims of six 175 ml ramekins). Fold each piece in half lengthways and fasten around the top edge of each ramekin with string or rubber bands. The paper should extend 5–6 cm above the rims.

2 Grate enough zest from the oranges to make 4 tablespoons loosely packed. Place the zest in a small stainless steel, glass, or enamel pan along with the Grand Marnier and the sugar. Simmer over low heat for 10–15 minutes, stirring frequently, until all the sugar is dissolved and the zest if translucent. Remove from heat.

3 Peel the oranges with a sharp knife, carefully removing all the white pith. Cut into segments and scrape out the pulp, removing the pips in the process.

4 Place the pulp in the bowl of a food processor along with the zest mixture and purée briefly. Place the mixture in a stainless steel, glass, or enamel pan. Sprinkle the gelatine over the mixture, and set it aside for a few minutes to soften. Then heat the mixture over medium-low heat, stirring constantly, until all of the gelatine is dissolved. Remove it from the heat, put it into a large bowl and cover it. Place the bowl in the refrigerator and chill, stirring occasionally, until the mixture mounds when dropped from a spoon (about 30 minutes).

5 In a small mixing bowl, whisk the egg whites with the salt substitute until they hold stiff peaks. Add the egg whites to the orange mixture. Using the same whisk, whip the low-fat cream in another bowl until it holds stiff peaks. Do not overbeat. Add the whipped low-fat cream to the other ingredients and gently fold together until thoroughly combined. Spoon the mixture into the ramekins and freeze for 2–3 hours, until set. Remove the paper collars before serving.

NUTRITIONAL VALUES

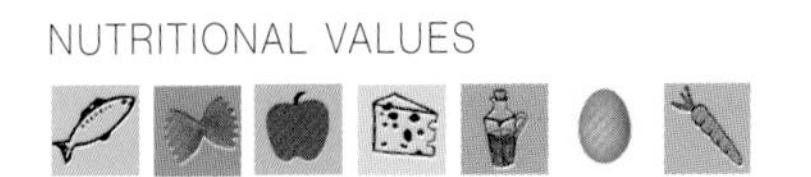

ICED BLACKCURRANT SOUFFLÉ

SERVES **6**

Fresh blackcurrants have a wonderfully refreshing taste, which is perfectly utlilized in this impressive looking soufflé.

450 g blackcurrants, hulled

150 g sugar

2 egg whites

100 g icing sugar, sifted

300 ml low-fat whipping cream

NUTRITIONAL VALUES

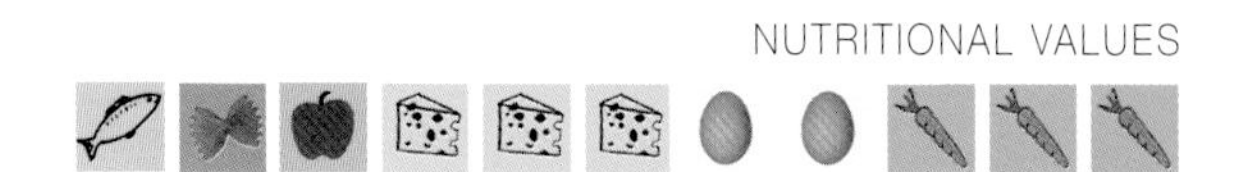

1 Wrap a double thickness of aluminium foil around a 1 litre soufflé dish to extend 5 cm above the rim of the dish. Cook the black currants with the sugar until soft, purée in a blender, and then strain. Allow to cool. Whisk the egg whites until stiff, then gradually whisk in the confectioners' sugar.

2 Whip the low-fat cream until softly stiff. Place the fruit purée in a large bowl and gradually fold in the egg white and low-fat cream. Pour into the prepared soufflé dish, level the surface, and freeze for several hours until solid. Remove the foil and serve.

STRAWBERRY TERRINE

SERVES **6–8**

This delightful dessert is so quick and simple to make. It is ideal for a dinner party.

450 g sugar substitute
zest of 1 orange, thinly grated
600 ml water
4 sachets powdered gelatine, about 44 g
2 tbsp Kirsch brandy
1 kg fresh strawberries, hulled and quartered

DECORATION
225 g fresh strawberries, halved

NUTRITIONAL VALUES

1. Put the sugar, orange zest and water into a pan and bring slowly to the boil, stirring occasionally. Boil for 5 minutes, then remove from the heat and allow to cool a little. Sprinkle on the gelatine crystals and stir well. Set aside to cool, but do not allow to set. Strain the syrup into a jug through a sieve lined with kitchen paper, and stir in the liqueur or brandy.

2. Rinse a 900 ml mould with cold water, and arrange the quartered strawberries to make a pattern. Slowly pour on the syrup, taking care not to displace the fruit. Cover the mould with foil and place it in the refrigerator for several hours or overnight.

3. To unmould the terrine, run a hot knife between the jelly and the mould and place a cloth rinsed in hot water over the base for no more than a few seconds. Place a serving plate over the mould, quickly invert the plate and the mould together and shake sharply to release the dessert.

4. Decorate the mould with fresh strawberries. You can hull the fruit if you wish, but it looks more decorative and provides a natural element of contrast if you do not.

CITRUS JELLY

SERVES **4**

A perfect way to follow a rich or substantial main dish – a refreshing three-fruit jelly set around a ring of orange segments and attractively decorated with lemon-scented geranium leaves.

6 oranges

1 lemon

200 ml water

1 sachet powdered gelatine, about 11 g

1 lime

clear honey, to taste

DECORATION

pistachio nuts

lemon-scented geranium leaves

NUTRITIONAL VALUES

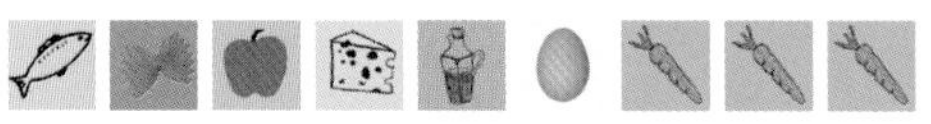

1. Using a potato peeler, remove just the peel of the oranges and the lemon, leaving the pith on the fruit. Place in a saucepan with 200 ml water, bring to the boil and simmer for 7–8 minutes. Segment the two oranges.

2. Sprinkle the gelatine over 3 tablespoons water and leave to swell for 5 minutes. Add the gelatine liquid to the pan off the heat, and stir to dissolve. Strain into a jug and discard the rind. Juice the remaining 4 oranges and lime then place in a measuring jug and add water to make 550 ml. Add to pan. Sweeten with honey if wished.

3. Pour the jelly into 4 individual sundae dishes and refrigerate to set, reserving 200 ml of the jelly.

4. Arrange the orange segments on top of each jelly and pour over the remaining liquid jelly. Refrigerate to set.

DAIRY MOULDS

SERVES **6**

A delicious low-fat version of the French coeur à la crème, *this dairy blend makes a light and delightful accompaniment to soft fruits of all kinds. It is also good with fresh dates or figs, or drizzled with honey and sprinkled with nuts.*

450 g low-fat cottage cheese

150 g low-fat double cream

150 g low-fat crème fraîche

3 tbsp warm water

1 sachet powdered gelatine, about 11 g

1. Sieve the cottage cheese into a bowl. Beat in the créme fraîche and low-fat double cream.

2. Pour the water into a small bowl, sprinkle on the gelatine, stir well and stand the bowl in a pan of warm water. Leave for about 5 minutes for the gelatine to dissolve. Pour the gelatine mixture into the cheese and beat well.

3. Spoon the cheese into 6 individual moulds. Heart-shaped ones are traditional, or you can improvise by using ramekin dishes or yoghurt pots covered with muslin and inverted. Stand the moulds on a wire rack over a plate and leave them to drain in the refrigerator overnight.

4. Turn out the moulds and serve the cheese well chilled.

NUTRITIONAL VALUES

LYCHEE SLAP

SERVES **4**

This oriental dessert can be served in a large dish in the centre of the table. The combination of delicate and strong flavours is a real treat.

1 medium jar Chinese stem ginger, drained

100 g can lychees

1 tbsp ginger wine

NUTRITIONAL VALUES

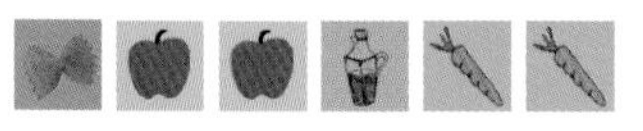

1 Insert a piece of the drained stem ginger into the centre of each lychee.

2 Mix the liquid from the stem ginger and the lychee syrup, and add the ginger wine. Pour the sauce over the stuffed lychees.

INDEX